Self-Determined Learning

Also Available From Bloomsbury

Meeting the Challenges of Change in Postgraduate Education,
edited by Trevor Kerry

Pedagogy and the University: Critical Theory and Practice,
Monica McClean

Transforming Learning in Schools and Communities:
The Remaking of Education for a Cosmopolitan Society,
edited by Bob Lingard, Jon Nixon and Stewart Ranson

Self-Determined Learning

Heutagogy in Action

Edited by
Stewart Hase and Chris Kenyon

BLOOMSBURY

LONDON • NEW DELHI • NEW YORK • SYDNEY

Bloomsbury Academic
An imprint of Bloomsbury Publishing Plc

50 Bedford Square	1385 Broadway
London	New York
WC1B 3DP	NY 10018
UK	USA

www.bloomsbury.com

Bloomsbury is a registered trademark of Bloomsbury Publishing Plc

First published 2013

© Stewart Hase, Chris Kenyon and Contributors, 2013

British Library Cataloguing-in-Publication Data
A catalogue record for this book is available from the British Library.

ISBN: HB: 978-1-4411-4277-1

Library of Congress Cataloging-in-Publication Data
Self-determined learning : heutagogy in action / edited by Stewart Hase, Chris Kenyon.
pages cm
Summary: "Explores how heutagogical approaches can be used in
a range of learning circumstances"– Provided by publisher.
Includes bibliographical references and index.
ISBN 978-1-4411-4277-1 (hardback) – ISBN 978-1-4411-0891-3 – ISBN 978-1-4411-9148-9
1. Learning, Psychology of. 2. Self-culture. I. Hase, Stewart, editor of compilation.
LB1060.S388 2013
370.15'23–dc23
2013015211

Design by Newgen Knowledge Works (P) Ltd., Chennai, India
Printed and bound in Great Britain

Contents

Illustrations

Figures

Tables

Boxes

Contributors

Lisa Marie Blaschke is program director of the Master of Distance Education and E-Learning (MDE) graduate program at Carl von Ossietzky Universität Oldenburg, Germany. She is also an associate professor (adjunct faculty) within the MDE partner graduate program at University of Maryland University College (UMUC) in Maryland, USA. Her research interests are in the areas of online collaborative learning and pedagogical application of Web 2.0 technologies. Lisa is also head of a communications consulting firm, which offers a wide range of distance education services, from e-learning design and development to project management.

Barbara A. Brandt is an educator, mathematician and mathematics consultant. As a mathematics consultant, she instructs teachers on the use of manipulative materials in mathematics education using a Piaget approach and emphasizing concept development from the concrete to the abstract. She is a proponent of 'play' as an instrument of learning. She is engaged in obtaining both a Master of Education and a Master of Science in Applied and Computational Mathematics at the University of Minnesota Duluth, USA.

Natalie Canning is a lecturer in education (early years) at the Open University, UK. Her background is in playwork and social work, supporting children to explore personal, social and emotional issues through play. She has published within the field of professional development in the early years, children's play and creative spaces. Her main research interest is children's empowerment in play. She has taught across a variety of early childhood undergraduate and postgraduate programmes and has edited Play and Practice in the Early Years Foundation Stage (2011), Reflective Practice in the Early Years (2010) and Implementing Quality Improvement and Change in the Early Years (2012).

Bob Dick is an independent scholar, an occasional academic and a freelance consultant in the fields of community and organizational change. In much of his current consulting he helps set up action learning programmes for leadership development, cultural change or the development of organizational resilience. In this work, and in his earlier work as a full time academic, his strong preference is to use highly participative and engaging processes. He lives in the leafy Western suburbs of Brisbane with the love of his life, Camilla.

Jane H. Eberle is an associate professor in Instructional Design and Technology in the Teachers College at Emporia State University (ESU), USA. She earned her PhD from Kansas State University, USA, and was an elementary school teacher in Manhattan, Kansas, USA, prior to joining the ESU faculty in 2003. She teaches Instructional Technology for Educators to preservice teachers and graduate courses in visual literacy, creativity in the classroom and integrating technology into the classroom. Her research interests include heutagogy, universal design for learning, technology integration and classroom teacher practices.

Roslyn Foskey is an adjunct lecturer in Education at the University of New England (UNE), Armidale, Australia. She has a particular interest in older adult learning and a background in applied rural social research. She was employed for many years with the multidisciplinary Institute for Rural Futures at UNE where she worked on projects examining farm succession, rural ageing, farming and retirement and older people and technology. She has often incorporated innovative and creative approaches to community engagement within her work, and is currently exploring an international collaboration with the 50+ ACT 11 STUDIO at Ryerson University, Canada.

Fred Garnett has worked with learning technologies since 1997 when he helped create the Lewisham TaLENT Community Grid for Learning. As Head of Community Programmes at Becta he lead on the UK's Community Access to Lifelong Learning programme, a £250 m digitally inclusive e-learning initiative, subsequently working on national policy development and on Participative Media Literacy with OFCOM. Since leaving Becta he has been a Visiting Research Fellow at the University of Sussex, UK, and the London Knowledge Lab, UK, advising on Digital Literacy. He is part of the Learner-Generated Contexts research group applying heutagogy to ambient learning in Manchester, UK, and self-accreditation in WikiQuals.

Stewart Hase is a psychologist who has been, variously, an academic, a therapist and an organizational consultant. He is now semi-retired and lives in a small fishing village on the north coast of New Souh Wales, Australia. Stewart spends his time writing, undertaking occasional organizational development projects, fishing, playing golf and travelling. He also talks about new approaches to learning whenever he can both nationally and internationally, and develops them concepts in his organizational consulting.

John Hurley is a mental health nurse, researcher, therapist and associate professor at Southern Cross University, Australia. John has a range of research projects and published work focusing on workforce development within health contexts. He has also previously published on heutagogy and adult learning approaches within the context of health education.

Chris Kenyon has worked as an adviser and consultant since 1980. Although much of his work has been in Australia, he has also worked in Saudi Arabia, USA, Malaysia, Thailand, Zambia and New Zealand. His clients have generally been government departments, though commercial clients have included several banks, grain exporters and power producers. His belief is that life is about learning, and he has at various times been a film producer, pilot, medical technician, academic, author (four books published) and ice cream vendor. He lives in a country house he designed and largely built himself about 30 km from Canberra, Australia.

Trevor Kerry taught in all phases of education before becoming a senior adviser with a UK local authority. He was formerly Professor of Education, Dean and Senior Vice-President at the College of Teachers, UK. He is the first Emeritus Professor of the University of Lincoln, UK, and Visiting Professor at Bishop Grosseteste University, Lincoln, UK. He has written and edited 30 education texts as well as hundreds of academic articles and journalistic pieces; and published a book of eco-history about a parson-naturalist. A keen photographer, he won the titles Honorary Master of Colour (International Colour Awards 2006, 2010) and Spider Fellow in Photography (2006, 2011).

Gavin R. Neilson is a lecturer in the School of Nursing and Midwifery, University of Dundee, UK. Gavin received his Doctor of Education from the University of Stirling, UK, and his thesis examined fifth- and sixth-year school pupils' perceptions of nursing as a career choice. He has published in the area of recruitment and perceptions of nursing as a career. Gavin's research interests include school pupils' reasons for choosing/not choosing nursing as a career; recruitment and retention; career socialization; images of nursing; career choice theory; and teaching and learning methodologies.

Ronan O'Beirne has spent 20 years working in public libraries and has been involved in many community-based learning projects. He was an early advocate of open learning resource use and worked on developments of metadata standards for learning opportunity information. His recent book From Lending to Learning; the Development and Extension of Public Libraries, which calls for public libraries to support informal lifelong learning, was published with excellent reviews. He is Director of Learning Development and Research at

Bradford College, UK. As a Fellow of the Chartered Institute of Library and Information Professionals he is actively involved in the library profession, chairing the national Library and Information Research Group and sitting on the editorial board of their international journal. In 2009 he was awarded the UK National Information Literacy practitioner of the year award. Ronan is completing a Doctor of Education EdD at the University of Sheffield, UK, looking at the relationship between academic libraries and research in the knowledge economy.

Mike Ramsay contributes extensively to undergraduate and postgraduate nursing courses, predominantly in mental health. He publishes widely in his field, mainly around older people, mental health nursing identity and education. His research interests are in nurse education, dementia and carer support. The latter reflects Mike's extensive experience in caring for older people's mental health in his 20-year clinical career prior to entering academia. He is currently undertaking a professional doctorate in education at the University of Dundee, UK.

Boon Hou Tay is currently the Director and Project Manager of IN Technology Pte Ltd. He pioneers three strategic research activities in the company, namely, Artificial Intelligence, Systems Engineering (via Action Research) and Datalink. The first involves development of an intelligent diagnostic expert system shell (DES) for implementing expert systems, embedded systems and prognostic solutions in automotive industries. The second involves the use of Action Research. For close to 14 years, he has been using Action Research as a meta-methodology for solving engineering and mathematical problems in the field of Systems Engineering. The third focuses on wireless and satellite communications.

Part One

The Fundamentals of Heutagogy

Introduction

Chris Kenyon and Stewart Hase

This book is not designed to be read chapter by chapter, rather, it is written for you to dip into, choosing the chapters that spark your interest. Our aim is to give you some idea of how self-determined learning is being adopted and adapted around the world. Heutagogy is not meant to replace other forms of learning, but it does offer an approach to learning that is quite different and that has been enthusiastically embraced by people working in academic education and in other areas of learning.

We start with two chapters that provide the details of how self-determined learning is used, and the theoretical concepts that underlie the approach. These chapters will be useful in appreciating the ideas put forward by other contributors to the book. However, if you are already familiar with the practicalities and the theory, you might want to jump in elsewhere in the book. Or, you might just like to confirm your understanding of what self-determined learning is all about.

In Chapter 3, Bob Dick writes that he has always had something of a learner-centred approach to education, but using action research and action learning, he has been able to provide learners with an approach that they find more rewarding. Bob describes how his approach was progressively implemented, and the benefits that ensued. Lisa Marie Blaschke provides examples of how Web 2.0 can be used to support self-determined learning. She suggests that future learning will increasingly use Web 2.0 and that self-determined learning lends itself particularly well to the use of information technology.

Trevor Kerry, in Chapter 5, describes how he came across the concept of self-determined learning, was attracted to it, and then used the approach in a postgraduate course. He provides a description of all the elements of the course and the way in which heutagogical principles were applied. Although the outcomes of the approach have been very positive, Trevor writes that he would like to make further improvements – the learning never ends. John Hurley, Mike

Ramsay and Gavin Neilson in Chapter 6 explain the use of heutagogy in the clinical component of undergraduate nursing education. The clinical experience opens up personal learning for students who can be given the opportunity to apply knowledge and skills in novel situations.

And for insights from a learner, Barbara Brandt's chapter provides a host of good reasons why self-determined learning can provide not just appeal, but more importantly, great satisfaction. She describes how, having been empowered by a self-determined learning, later being exposed to a more traditional approach was disappointing. As an experienced teacher, Barbara now sees the need for more teachers to adopt a heutagogical approach, believing that both they and the learners will thereby benefit.

Fred Garnett offers something quite different in his chapter – he looks at how the Beatles developed in stages to finally entering a heutagogical phase of their musicianship. Fred's knowledge of the Beatles is encyclopaedic and so his analysis of their learning and development is not only fascinating but well informed. In the next chapter Fred teams with Ronan O'Beirne in Chapter 9 to describe a community learning programme which moves along the pedagogy-andragogy-heutagogy continuum. They find that e-learning offers great opportunities for self-determined learning and will probably be vital in future learning programmes.

Jane Eberle also thinks that e-learning offers opportunities for adopting a heutagogical approach to learning, but says that the approach can work equally well with face-to-face learning. Her argument is that by providing the right learning environment, it is not only the learners who greatly benefit, but the facilitators of the learning also come to appreciate the extension of their own knowledge. Stewart Hase extends this approach in face-to-face learning, by describing how he has used self-determined learning in what would normally be considered a 'teaching' situation – running training courses. He shows how, given the freedom to learn, participants become actively involved in their learning, rather than being merely passive 'trainees'.

Natalie Canning writes about her research on the UK Early Years Professional Status (EYPS) programme, which is designed to give formal qualifications to people working with young children. She describes how the elements of self-determined learning, such as complexity, motivation and emotion can play an integral part in a learning programme, and how graduates should be able to adopt the approach in their subsequent work with youngsters. Boon Hou Tay in Chapter 13 offers a fascinating look into how he sees the pedagogy-andragogy-heutagogy continuum applying in the way we look at and understand the world around us. He argues that heutagogy gives us a greater desire and capability for learning, so that we see learning as an ever-open door, and not something that is closed and completed.

Ros Foskey describes her work with older men living in rural communities, to enhance their health and well-being through the use of interactive theatre. She shows how giving people the opportunity to determine what they want to learn and be involved in, not only increases their sense of self-worth but has consequent health benefits.

Finally we look at the future for self-determined learning. We consider that, given its adoption around the world and its ready fit with e-learning (as well as in more traditional learning situations), a useful future is assured.

1

Heutagogy Fundamentals

Chris Kenyon and Stewart Hase

Summary

This chapter provides an overview of the various elements that make up the heutagogical approach to learning. It includes information on why heutagogy seems to be successful for many learners, and describes the steps to be taken when heutagogy is introduced into a formal education system. The benefits and challenges of the approach are also discussed along with helpful hints. Other chapters in this book describe in more detail many of the elements in this chapter. Here we provide a broad picture of what heutagogy is and how it is applied.

Introduction

Welcome to the world of heutagogy, or as it is defined, 'self-determined learning' (Hase and Kenyon, 2000). The essence of heutagogy is that in some learning situations, the focus should be on what and how the learner wants to learn, not on what is to be taught. Hence this approach is very different from the more formal and traditional way of 'teaching' people. In heutagogy the educational process changes from being one in which the learned person (teacher, tutor, lecturer) pours information into the heads of learners, to one in which the learner chooses what is to be learned and even how they might learn it. It represents a change from teacher-centred learning to learner-centred learning. In the heutagogical approach the 'learned' person takes on more of a role as a facilitator or guide as to how the desired learning might take place, and if formal assessment of the learning is required, then the 'learned' person assists in determining what will be an appropriate means of assessment.

There are further elements to this approach to learning, such as the question of how the learning is going to take place, and how the learner is to be guided in their learning. Also, we need to be sure that the desired learning is within the capabilities and maturity level of the potential learner. An average 10-year-old might find themselves unreasonably challenged, no matter how much they might want to learn about existential theory! That said, one of the inherent benefits of the heutagogical approach that many learners have already discovered is that their learning capabilities are considerably enhanced through using this approach. Hence the challenge of learning something that, conventionally, might be perceived as being outside their capabilities, may in fact develop and extend learners' capabilities. This has particular relevance given today's emphasis on lifelong learning.

Examples of heutagogy in action

Let's look at an example. Bronwyn is studying tourism and hospitality, and one of the subjects in her final year is Hotel Management. While Bronwyn could attend lectures and sit the usual exam at the end of the year, she prefers to take a different approach to her learning. She negotiates with her lecturer to spend two months working as an employee in different roles in a large hotel – she wants to see 'management' from the other side. She sits down with her lecturer and plans her assignment: together they agree on how often she will report her progress, identify appropriate learning resources, engage with content and how a final assessment will be made. They might agree that the assessment will be a lengthy paper on her experiences, indicating how management theories stack up in the practical world of hotel management. She might support her paper with a diary kept during the work period. She might give a presentation to a small group of academic staff. If assessment is required, then its format would be determined by agreement between the learner and her guide. If the subject can be measured by the appropriate length of time spent 'studying', then two months of day and night shifts in a major hotel could well be sufficient for this purpose.

So, in this case of Bronwyn having to satisfy an academic requirement, there are the following elements to the planned learning: guided choice of topic, guided approach to the proposed learning, agreement on reporting progress and agreement on the content and method of final assessment. It seems simple enough, and can be so, but there may also be some challenges in adopting self-determined learning, and these are discussed a little later in this chapter.

Let's take another example, but this one does not concern learning for academic purposes. Owen has just retired and has been attending lectures on the history of the Middle East. He is fascinated by the very long journeys that people made by camel and on foot in the eighteenth centry: how did they do it, how did they survive? He reads a lot, and searches for yet more information on the internet. Finally he asks his lecturer at the University of the Third Age, or maybe the writer of one of the books he has read, to advise on how he can learn more. Perhaps the advice is to go to the Middle East and experience a journey for himself. Off he goes, trekking through the edges of deserts, stopping in small villages, wearing traditional clothing and eating local foods. On the way, he occasionally comes across the ruins of a small fort inside which travellers used to pitch their tents. He is intrigued by the structures – where did the stones come from and how was a fort built? On returning home he might develop an interest in archeology or the Arabic language or geology. Most probably he would seek guidance on how he can learn more – before he heads off again.

In both of these examples, the learners have a strong desire to gain knowledge and understanding in particular areas. This search for understanding may come from a desire to expand their knowledge, or from having questions to which they do not yet have the answers. It is this strong motivation that is at the heart of the learning. As young children we often ask hundreds of questions – possibly to the dismay of our parents. In fact young children are very capable learners. But as we get older our education system seems to suppress our wish to ask questions, by telling us what we need to know. What we need to know has been determined through decades of teaching and development, and is based on what are the perceived needs of the average learner at any particular age: generally there is no room for satisfying individual learning desires. And yet we are no longer living in an industrial age but in an information age: it is our motivation to learn more, to gain ever more information and to find answers to our questions that underlie the effectiveness of learner-centred learning.

Motivation and desire are the emotional commitment to learning which makes the heautagogical approach so highly successful. There is evidence that many heutagogical learners not only achieve good academic results, but also go on to further studies. Where heutagogy has been used outside academia, there is anecdotal evidence that learners have enjoyed the learning experience, and have gained increased confidence in their ability to learn: not surprisingly, this has also led to many people wanting to undertake further learning. Barbara Brandt describes the experience from the learner's perspective in more detail in Chapter 7.

Learning outcomes

The reason for the successful learning appears fairly simple – the joy and the satisfaction from learning what was needed and wanted. But there is probably an associated reason for success – the amount of time spent in the learning process. Our experience has been that learners can become so fascinated and absorbed by their learning that they spend far more time than is formally required for any assessment purpose. They spend hours and hours learning, pursuing what fascinated them because they want to; the learning is no longer seen in terms of a 'requirement' but becomes a pleasurable and inherently rewarding experience. It doesn't matter – within reason – how long the learning takes, the learners tend to be absorbed in their learning and are less aware of time constraints. For those learners in a non-academic environment, the time spent learning can perhaps extend for ever.

A second successful outcome for learners who are exposed to a heutagogical approach to learning, is that they develop the desire and the skills to be better and more active learners. While we initially thought that this continuation of a drive for learning was based on the high level of satisfaction from previous learning (people enjoyed their learning and so wanted to repeat the experience) there are probably at least two other factors at work. First, learners develop learning capability, they learn how to learn. They become increasingly skilled in research methods, in undertaking relevant practical work and in seeking information from people around the world (rather than just those in their immediate environment). They also become proficient in planning their learning. The second factor is neurological. It seems that while learning is taking place, brain plasticity allows for existing neural pathways to be enhanced, and also for new pathways to be established – the learners' brains become more efficient. While further research would be needed to establish if and how such brain development occurs, current evidence suggests that the brain can develop increased capability. It is probable that learning something may lead to unpredictable outcomes for the learner, as they make myriad connections in their brain and start asking new questions and seeing the world in a new way. This change in the way we see things is discussed in more detail in Chapter 2.

Applicability to most learners

Although the theory and practice of heutagogy was first developed for working with learners at postgraduate level, it is clear from the enthusiastic response to the approach that heutagogy has a far more widespread application. It is being used in primary and secondary education, and in commercial organizations where the focus is on learning and development. It is being used online, and it is being used in situations where no assessment is needed and people learn simply for the joy of learning. However, heutagogy should not be considered as being the prime method of learning for all situations. There still is an essential role for the more didactic, pedagogical, forms of teaching where the learner must develop certain skills or knowledge in order to get started in a completely new area. A medical student cannot learn surgery in a completely self-determined way, a welder must learn and practice appropriate skills before firing up his (or her) torch as a professional welder. In Chapter 2 we see how the teaching process moves from pedagogy and andragogy and then to heutagogy, as the learner matures. Heutagogy is not simply an alternative to pedagogy and androgogy, but a useful extension that provides a valuable and different approach to learning.

Elements

Let's look now at the various elements that are part of adopting a heutagogical approach to learning. Some of these elements will not be needed in situations of non-formal education.

1. *Approval.* Depending on the level of autonomy granted to teaching staff, someone, or some body, may need to approve the use of heutagogical approach to learning before it is implemented in a curriculum. The body might be an academic board, and the individual decision makers could be heads of departments, senior staff or even lecturers. In corporate training the consultant/facilitator may need to convince a CEO or training manager of what initially appears to be a rather innovative approach. In many circumstances, as you'll see in the rest of this book, heutagogy can be implemented in part, and in areas outside of formal education settings requires no approval.
2. *Facilitators.* People who are going to facilitate the progress of the learners are best described as facilitators or guides. Their role is to ensure that learners

are provided with relevant guidance to ensure that the learning outcomes are optimized. This interaction with the learner can also provide learning for the facilitator. Our experience has been that lecturers and teachers who take on the role of facilitator can perhaps find such work quite demanding, but also their own interest in and joy of learning is rekindled as they try more exciting learner-centric methods. Clearly, any lecturers and teachers who are firmly committed to their lectures and lesson plans are going to feel challenged by a suggestion that heutagogy offers a more appropriate approach to learning in the twenty-first century. Some will stick to their established teaching methods, some will half-heartedly attempt to adopt heutagogy, and perhaps some will see the benefits of the new approach and fully embrace it.

3. *Choice.* Learners, as would be expected, range widely in the extent of the learning they wish to undertake. Some want to gain in-depth understanding of highly complex areas, while others have more narrowly defined areas for learning. Many know the sort of area they want to learn about, for example eco-tourism, container shipping or local geology, but need to find a particular aspect to focus upon. This is where the facilitator comes in: their role is to help the learner more clearly define what they want to learn. The facilitator will consider three things: relevance, achievability and level. What the learner is seeking to learn about must be relevant to the course of study being undertaken, the topic needs to be appropriate and not merely something that the learner thinks is interesting. How much time is available to the learner to undertake their work? It is important to establish the scope of the proposed learning so that a successful outcome can be achieved.

That said, our experience has been that the majority of learners do spend far more time on their work than 'officially' required when pursuing a topic of their choosing, many saying that they do not regard the extra time as 'work' rather that it is something they enjoy doing. Finally, level. While a primary school student may want to learn about the disappearance of dinosaurs, a postgraduate student could be expected to learn about a far more complex subject – although of course, the disappearance of dinosaurs may have complex geological, environmental and biological elements. The choice of learning topic is thus scaled to the abilities of the learner, the time available and the complexity of the topic.

There is also choice about the way learning might occur. The traditional teacher-centric approach to learning has been that the teacher chooses both content and process. Here, the learner might want to apply knowledge and skills in a novel context, work with others, undertake interviews or other research, or try and create something new.

4. *Agreement.* The learner and facilitator agree on a time frame for the learning, the methodologies to be used, the frequency of reviews of progress and the form of a final assessment – should one be required. While a verbal agreement may suffice with some learners, experience suggests that having a documented agreement is a good idea. The learner can then be reminded of their responsibilities, should the plan of learning go off track. This is not to say that the agreement should be a formal and binding contract. On the contrary, there needs to be some flexibility so that if circumstances change, the learning programme can adapt accordingly. We have found that the most frequent change is that learners have found one aspect of their learning that is of particular relevance or interest to them, and they want to amend the focus of their learning. Provided that the new focus is still achievable and at the right level, then there should be a green light to continue the learning.

5. *Review.* The heutagogical definition of learning assumes that as people are presented with new knowledge and skills there is a possibility that the learner will develop new insights unknown to the facilitator: it is this acquisition of insights that we define as learning. The learner, then, has new questions, challenges and possibly further avenues to pursue. Thus, it is vital for the facilitator to find out at regular intervals what progress has been made and what any new needs might be. The review session involves more than a general question such as "How is your work progressing?' It is a deeper process that embeds the learning experience associated with the tenets of double loop learning and action learning. Bob Dick describes this in more detail in Chapter 3.

   In short, however, review sessions might involve agreed meetings with the facilitator as individuals or groups, face-to-face or using available technology. In the latter case it can be synchronous or asynchronous using blogs, Wikis or similar approaches. Review can also be embedded in the learning experience by having participants engage in group and individual reflection that results in a reportable output. This latter aspect is discussed in Chapter 11.

6. *Assessment.* At the end of the defined learning period, if there is a requirement for assessment, then this will be in the form agreed to at the start of the learning. Common forms of assessment have included papers, reports, presentations to colleagues and briefings to academic staff.

Assessment is discussed further in the later section on the challenges of the learner-centred approach.

7. *Feedback.* While this is not a requirement as such, experience indicates that an informal discussion where the learner and facilitator exchange ideas and experiences can be most beneficial. The learner may talk about the challenges faced (and overcome) and the learner's new capabilities, while the facilitator gains useful information on ways of guiding future learners. This activity can be done in groups and can take the place of a didactic lecture or a planned group activity.

This exchange of experiences generally confirms the value of learner-centred learning, while also offering insights as to how future learning, by both parties, might be approached.

Benefits of the approach

The benefits that accrue from a self-determined approach to learning are significant, not only for the individual learner, but most probably for society as a whole.

The obvious benefit is that an individual learns what they have chosen to learn, not just what is dictated by a curriculum. In effect the curriculum is the starting point, a springboard. The satisfaction in this process is enormous, not only from the learning that takes place, but also because the learner experiences their personal empowerment in becoming directly responsible for their learning as an active rather than a passive learner. From these core benefits, experience shows that another benefit commonly occurs, and that is a learner's increased capability. In this context, we mean that the learner comes to understand more about the learning process, and becomes more adept at learning for themselves. They become confident in using different approaches and sources to advance their learning, and know how and where to look, not only for information but for experiences that will contribute to, or enhance, their learning. In turn, this increased capability often results in learners continuing to learn more and more, probably because of the sense of satisfaction in so doing, but possibly also because their brains are now more fully developed in undertaking learning. A further advantage to self-determined learning is that, usually, it is not time-bound. In other words, the learner is able to choose the time when they wish the learning to start, and to some extent, the length of time during which the learning will take place. Of course, outside the world of formal education, there is often no limit on when someone can begin their learning, nor any constraints on the amount of time taken to achieve that learning. So the flexibility of the approach can provide learners with greater opportunities than the more traditional approaches to learning.

For those who guide the learning of self-determined learners, there can also be new forms of satisfaction. One form is in the nature of directly and positively influencing a learner, not by directing them or lecturing to them, but by listening to the learner's ideas and then offering guidance appropriate to their desired path of learning. Further satisfaction may come from the establishment of a direct relationship with the learner; this will often have a strength and positivity that is not found in more formal approaches to teaching and learning. Thirdly, these facilitators of learning usually find themselves also learning, not only because they realize there is more to learn, but also because the enjoyment of directly facilitating learning engenders a desire for more learning on their part.

On a wider scale, there are benefits to society through having people who are more knowledgeable, more skilled and more capable of learning. As the world continues to change at an ever-increasing rate, society needs more and more people who are capable learners. And as the approach is not limited to one area of learning, it can be applied to formal and informal learning, for all ages.

Challenges of the approach

The primary challenge, as with all significant changes to the ways in which things are accepted as being 'properly' done, is for those involved in education and learning to accept that heutagogy does not represent a threat to conventional methodologies, but is a highly desirable development beyond current approaches. Self-determined learning does not undermine established systems of education, rather it offers those who desire to follow it, and those who wish to facilitate it, an opportunity to learn in a most fulfilling and satisfying way.

A second obstacle may be found in those who see education as being the process by which information and appropriate experiences are provided to learners. This view of education may be held by the individuals who provide the education, as well as by those who control the institutions in which the education takes place. Some educators see self-determined learning as a threat to their status as learned persons who bestow their knowledge on learners; this reaction might be thought quite understandable. However, what heutagogy offers is for these educators to not only help other people learn through working as facilitators, but also the chance for greater learning (and kudos perhaps) for themselves.

A third obstacle is time. There is a suggestion that while heutagogy is all very well in principle, in practical terms it is difficult to adopt, and that is because it is more time consuming than the more traditional ways of teaching. But is that the case? We have only heard this view from people who do not wish to adopt the self-determined learning approach. None of those organizations around the globe that have adopted the heutagogical approach have mentioned that it requires more time of the facilitators. This may indicate that even if any extra time is required, it is not significant, or perhaps is considered to be of little consequence given the benefits to learners that accrue from this approach.

Non-universality is a fourth obstacle. While self-determined learning approaches are widely welcomed in several countries and by groups ranging from those involved in primary education to those in tertiary education and in informal learning groups, it does not purport to be the one ideal method of learning. For a variety of reasons, more traditional approaches to learning will be appropriate in some circumstances. For example where skills and knowledge need to be taught before the learner can be considered safe to use them; we would not want to be represented in a court of law by someone learning law, or be operated on by a would-be surgeon. There is also a need to take into account the personality of the learner; less confident learners may well feel that self-determined learning is too great a challenge, and they may prefer to sit and be taught in the traditional manner. Given the strength of some traditions, it is probable that in those societies where education is conducted in a very traditional didactic manner, and where teachers are seen as the fonts of knowledge, that the heutagogical approach will not easily find acceptance, except perhaps as an interesting concept.

Next comes culture. There are inevitably difficulties in implementing heutagogical approaches to learning in those cultures, which have a great respect for centuries-long, traditional teaching methods, and where there is a belief in the important status of teachers and older people. In such cultures, even asking questions of the teacher would be frowned upon, and hence allowing young people to have any say in what they learn is most unlikely to happen. And lest we jump to the conclusion that such cultures might mainly be found in Africa and Asia, let us not forget that there are many august institutions of learning in Europe and the Americas, where hundreds of years of tradition still demand that would-be learners gain their knowledge from those chosen to educate them. Allowing for a flexible curriculum and offering assessment forms other than exams will be, for the time being, too great a challenge for cultures where tradition is respected and revered. However, as the world grows smaller, and as information spreads ever more rapidly around the globe, perhaps there will be a more universal recognition of the value of heutagogy in learning.

The final obstacle can be that of assessment. If an institution has always relied on examinations as a way of assessing a learner's knowledge, then moving to a different form of assessment may be seen as a threat; it may also be seen as an opportunity, depending on the outlook of the decision makers. If there is a requirement for formal assessment, then this is usually in the form agreed to by the learner and the facilitator at the start of the learning assignment. It is possible that during the learning assignment the focus of the learning may change slightly, and hence the agreed method of assessment might also need to change. There needs to be a recognition that the form of assessment needs to be appropriate to the learning that has taken place. Should a 10,000-word paper be required? Is a one-hour presentation to fellow students and interested staff appropriate? Is a report to the external organization in which the learning was pursued needed? This range of options may cause unease to those who have always used exams for assessment. But our argument would be that choosing an assessment method that best fits the learning provides a more appropriate indicator of learning than does an exam. Moreover, as staff, educators are trusted to mark exams objectively. When staff become facilitators of learning there is no reason for them to provide less objective assessments of the learning that has taken place. In short, there is a need to move from the 'one size fits all' approach that examinations provide, to an approach of 'what is the best fit for this learner?'

The next chapter discusses the underlying theories, which underpin the self-determined learning approach, and also the theories that help explain some of the reasons for heutagogy being adopted in many different levels of learning and many different areas around the world.

2

The Nature of Learning

Stewart Hase and Chris Kenyon

Summary

This chapter will do two things. It will, for the uninitiated, summarize the origins of heutagogy and the theories from which it was derived. At the same time we will have a look at more recent work and thinking from authors around the globe and see what they have discovered through using or thinking about heutagogical principles. The main theme of the chapter is that people are naturally very efficient learners and that we can more effectively make use of this fact in our current education and training systems.

Origins and influences

The power to learn

Heutagogy has come a long way since its initial inception over a bottle of wine and notes written on a napkin in a restaurant in 2000 (Hase, 2002, 2009; Hase and Kenyon, 2000, 2003, 2007, 2010; Kenyon and Hase, 2010). Don't most good ideas happen this way? The discussion came about as a result of a general dissatisfaction with the way in which education was being conducted in universities. We thought that, despite the role of higher education to foster our brightest minds and to expand the frontiers of knowledge, teaching was primarily a pedagogic, teacher-centric, activity. To our way of thinking, teaching in our universities needed to be more aspirational.

Like other humanists such as Carl Rogers (1969) we believe that the power to learn is firmly in the hands of the learner and not the teacher. We also recognize, as have Russell Ackoff and Daniel Greenberg (2008), that humans are from early childhood really adept learners and that much of the education system confuses learning with teaching. In fact, there is sometimes so much confusion that it can interfere with people's natural ability to explore, ask questions, make connections and to learn. This humanistic view of how people learn has been coined as student-centred learning (Rogers, 1969) or, more recently, learner-centred learning (Armstrong, 2012; Graves, 1993; Long 1990) as opposed to teacher-centric approaches.

Recently I was asked to talk to a group of trainers working for the NSW Rural Fire Service in Australia. It was their annual conference and they were interested in finding more exciting ways to train their 70,000 or so volunteers in the various competencies required to fight fires. I showed a picture of an ancient fire engine from the end of the nineteenth century but suggested that they think of it as a new piece of fire equipment. A teacher-centric approach to learning about this new equipment would be to show some pictures to the group, go through the manual, demonstrate the required skills and then have the group practice until the required competency might be attained. A more learner-centric approach and rather more naturalistic, would be to let the group go play with the machinery and leave the manual on the seat. The facilitator can play an important role by watching and making sure that all is safe and intervening if someone is going to initiate a catastrophic event. Everyone agreed that, indeed, the group would work it out for themselves.

Unfortunately, as Ackoff and Greenberg (2008) describe so elegantly, humans are hijacked very early in life by an educational system that was designed in the industrial revolution to educate workers to make the industrial wheel go around. Thus, education has become a commodity and the curriculum, chiselled in stone, is delivered by 'experts' from on high. Assessment becomes the key for opening doors and teaching is geared to providing the key. The needs and motivations of the learner and, more importantly, what is happening in their brain is of secondary importance, if it is of any importance at all.

The late Fred Emery was a little more scathing in his assessment of the education system (1974, p. 1) when he said that, 'School pokes your eyes out. University teaches you braille and postgraduate education is speed-reading in braille.' Less controversially, a number of educationalists have questioned the assumptions that underpin common educational practice and the need for approaches that recognize the complexity of the relationship between the learner, the curriculum and learning (e.g. Davis et al., 2000; Doll, 1989; Doolittle, 2000; Sumara and Davis, 1997). Current education practice places the process and outcomes of learning in the hands of the teacher who determines what is to be taught and how it is to be taught when, in fact, it needs to be in the hands of the learner (Coughlan, 2004).

Given these beliefs about people's ability to learn and an education and training system that disempowers rather than empowers, we decided on the term self-determined learning to describe this innate power of people to learn as an alternate view. Chris, the linguist that he is, then manipulated the Greek word for self, ηαυτος, and came up with the word heutagogy: the study of self-determined learning.

Humanism and constructivism

Heutagogy is underpinned by the assumptions of two key philosophies: humanism and constructivism. As mentioned above, the idea of the learner being central to the educational process is a humanistic concept. Carl Rogers later adapted his client-centred approach to psychotherapy (1951) to education (1969) in what was termed student-centred learning. Similarly, constructivism places the learner at the heart of the educational experience (e.g. Bruner, 1960; Dewey, 1938; Freire, 1972, 1995; Piaget, 1973; Vygotsky, 1978). Constructivism is based on the notion that people construct their own version of reality using past experience and knowledge, and their current experience. Thus, the learner is creative, actively involved in their learning and there is a dynamic rather than passive relationship between the teacher and the learner.

Constructivism challenged educators to let go of some of the structure in what they did and allow greater dynamism into the curriculum. Constructivism led to a rise in the popularity of designing experiential learning as a means for loosening this control. However, in our view, it did not have the impact on lessening the control of the learning experience by the teacher and hence education at all levels has remained teacher-centric. While many constructivist approaches cleverly engage the learner in experience and active learning, the teacher is still actively designing the learning task and process. In learner-centred learning tasks become less specific as control of learning is taken over by the learner (Coomey and Stephenson, 2001).

Andragogy (Knowles, 1980, 1986) is also based on humanism and constructivism and was central to the original paper we wrote in 2000. Andragogy was important because it provided an alternate to pedagogical approaches to teaching towards those more suitable for adults. Knowles was interested in the motivational aspects of adult learning and emphasized the previous experience of the learner, relevance, problems versus content and involvement of the learner in the learning process. The idea of the self-directed learner can be sheeted back to Andragogy. However, while context might be in the hands of the learner, the teacher is still largely in control of process and task. Unfortunately, some students of heutagogy refer to it as self-directed rather than self-determined learning: the two are perhaps related but quite different.

Finally, Argyris and Schon's (1978) notion of double-loop learning influenced our thinking about heutagogy and others have since associated the two concepts (e.g. Blaschke, 2012; Canning, 2010; Canning and Callan, 2010). Double-loop learning often occurs spontaneously and involves internally challenging our deepest values, beliefs and ways of knowing. While it is difficult to change any of these schema that drive human behaviour, it is at this level that the deepest learning occurs.

Reconceptualizing learning

The science of learning, discovering how people learn, as apposed to the philosophy of learning and education that goes back to Egyptian times, can be sheeted back to around the tenth-century. However, it is only recently that advances in neuroscience and the capacity to investigate the functioning of the brain have really enabled us to see what happens when we learn. In the past ten years our understanding has risen exponentially.

Commonly used definitions of learning have failed to keep pace with these advances in neuroscience and appear to be rather outmoded (Hase, 2010). Learning is often referred to as knowledge being gained through study, instruction or scholarship or the act of gaining knowledge. Many accepted psychological definitions refer to learning as being the result of any change in behaviour that results from experience. Discussions about learning mostly concern the education process rather than what happens in the brain of the learner – where learning really takes place.

It's important to establish at this point that we are not attempting a neurological reductionist explanation of learning. Clearly learning is a complex interaction of myriad influences including genes, neurophysiology, physical state, social experience and psychological factors. However, we suggest that understanding what is happening in the brain when we learn might provide important new insights into what is happening to the learner in the education or training experience.

When we learn something, networks of neurons are established that can later be accessed, what we call memory (e.g. Benfenati, 2007). Laying down larger and larger numbers of pathways creates an increasingly complex matrix (Willis, 2006). Thus, old and new pathways influence each other in potentially quite dramatic ways through a process of activation and association (Khaneman, 2011). It appears that humans seek to make patterns from their experience. Furthermore, it is hard to predict just what the effect of this pattern making from the mix of new and old learning might be. We might be aiming for a simple change in behaviour, a new competency perhaps. But the learner may end up making a whole bunch of cognitive leaps and end up seeing the world in completely different ways: ways not necessarily defined by the curriculum, which now becomes a constraint.

Thus, every brain is different. Our experiences mean that each person will selectively focus on different issues, concerns and applications of the things they are learning. They will be asking different questions in their minds, testing their own hypotheses, making their own conclusions as a result. John Medina in 'Brain Rules' (2008a) gives a great example of the neuroscience underpinning the above assertion. The part of the cerebral cortex for the use of the fingers of the left hand in a right-handed violinist is extremely dense with cells. Presumably this is the result of practice. People who do not play the violin do not have this density in the same place but presumably have denser areas elsewhere depending on what their areas of interest might be. So, the response of the individual to new information, to new experiences will vary a great deal due to this unconscious selection. In fact, it may take years before a person has that 'ah, ah', moment. This all questions the fixed curriculum, didactic teaching, teacher-directed learning and many of the methods we currently use.

The notion of brain plasticity recently popularized by Doidge (2007) also provides some fascinating insights into how people learn. More importantly these insights have led to the development of highly focused techniques being used to target very specific areas of the brain. Neuroscience research shows that the more we actually 'do' with a new piece of learning the greater the number of neuronal pathways that are established and cemented in place through the development of matrices of dendrites mediated by the release of neurotrophins (Willis, 2006). This supports previous well-known evidence that an enriched environment leads to increased development of the brain (Rosenzweig et al., 1962) and this finding is used in a number of educational contexts.

Exploration is far more effective for learning than using rote methods or passive processes. It is also interesting that the more satisfying, engaging and perhaps exciting the education process, the more internally reinforcing it is to the learner through the release of dopamine (Willis, 2006). There are parts of the brain that are responsible for watching others, forming hypopheses, testing assumptions and generally exploring (Gopnik et al., 2000). These skills and the relevant brain activity is seen in children – they are great learners.

Repetition using different senses, application and providing context or at least finding out what the learner's context might be are critical to learning. In fact the more elaborately we experience something more likely we are to learn it (Craik and Tulving, 1975; Gabrielli et al., 1996; Grant et al., 1998; Hasher and Zacks, 1984; LeDoux, 2002; Medina, 2008b). The converse is also true. The human attention span has been shown to be limited to about ten minutes when stimulation is low and there is an absence of activity (Johnstone and Percival, 1976; Middendorf and Kalish, 1996). Humans are built to be active, to do things, to apply, to explore and to be curious. They are not designed to sit still and pay attention to the same stimuli for long periods – this induces a state of trance, as most hypnotists know.

Our understanding of learning can best be summarized by Sumara and Davis (1997, p. 107) as: '. . . a process of organizing and reorganizing one's own subjective world of experience, involving the simultaneous revision, reorganization and reinterpretation of past, present and projected actions and conceptions'. Learning results in a whole new set of questions to ask, based on their new understanding, not only different from their colleagues but also outside the curriculum, if not well beyond it. These new questions provide a motivation to learn. Perhaps the example below will illustrate what is meant by this.

Until 1697 all known swans were white. Nobody had seen a black swan, so in English poetry the idea of a black swan represented the impossible. In that fateful year Willem de Vlamingh, a Dutch explorer, discovered black swans in what was later to become Western Australia. Suddenly, the whole idea of swans changed, as did the metaphor for impossibility. The change eventually led Nassim Taleb in 2004 to write about black swan events. These are unpredictable things that happen, good and bad, that have profound effects on the world. They are things we often fail to plan for and, in fact, we cannot prepare for, except by building resilience in people and in organizations. Taleb's novel conceptualization of the black swan leads to a complete rethinking of what we mean by strategic planning by focusing on building capacity for dealing with uncertainty.

Heutagogy also draws on the notion of capability (e.g. Stephenson, 1996; Stephenson and Weil, 1992) by distinguishing between the acquisition of knowledge and skills or competencies and the deeper cognitive processes described above. Capability involves using competencies in new contexts and challenging situations. It is about the unknown and the future, rather than the routine. In demonstrating capability the person is making a host of new neuronal connections, creating new hypotheses and testing them mentally and physically, in understanding the best way to proceed. At the same time, capability requires the learner to have a high degree of self-efficacy in their ability to learn and access appropriate resources. Capable people also recognize the need to work with others to deal with new and changing circumstances. Competencies are the building blocks of learning but our life experiences, serendipity, challenges, the unknown future, things outside our control, make us do more with these building blocks.

Thus, we propose that there are perhaps two levels of learning: the acquisition of knowledge and skills on the one hand and, on the other, this more complex neuronal activity. Pedagogy and andragogy describe the educational activities used in the development of competence, the acquisition of knowledge and skills (Tay and Hase, 2004) as learners struggle with new concepts and ideas. Andragogical techniques are used as the learner makes connections with their previous experience. Tay and Hase (2004) studied engineers and business managers undertaking a PhD using an action research approach. With backgrounds based in technical and scientific research, action research was a completely new concept. Tay and Hase found that the students moved from pedagogy, with a high reliance on the supervisors, to andragogy as they started to make sense of how to apply action research to their life experience.

They then found that reliance on the supervisor diminished and the process became more learner-centric or heutagogic. There is less predictability about the task and process. Here the needs of the learner and their motivation may change rapidly as new connections are made, novel applications are tested and concepts are redesigned to suit individual needs. This higher-level learning may not be, '. . . necessarily in concert with the aims of the teacher or the curriculum' (Hase, 2009, p. 46).

While this study clearly showed a shift from dependent learner to self-determined learner we do not completely agree with some writers (Anderson, 2006; Luckin et al., 2011) who suggest that pedagogy, andragogy and heutagogy (PAH) necessarily lie on a continuum – the PAH Continuum (Luckin et al., 2011). This continuum assumes that the learner moves from pedagogy to heutagogy depending on their level of sophistication. This may be the case (as described by Tay and Hase (2004)) but is not always so. For example, children are very competent learners until process and content are pulled from their grasp by schooling, no matter their level of sophistication.

Emotion and motivation

Studies of the human brain also demonstrate the important role of emotions in learning, memory and decision-making (e.g. Damasio, 2003; Dolcos et al., 2004; Medina, 2008a). The driver of emotions, the amygdala, is connected to areas of the cortex responsible for higher-order cognitive functions and learning. Thus, emotions affect learning, as they do analysis, decision-making and action. As Hase (2009, p. 46) states:

> It is also clear that there are complex interactions between learning and emotions in that the latter may make learning more indelible (Ingleton, 1999). Learning, then, is probably enhanced by excitement and enjoyment, and when there is a gap in understanding that creates curiosity, confusion or a gentle unease. Thus, it is the questions that the learning experience raises rather than the provision of answers that are the primary concern of heutagogy.

It is our contention that it is the role of the learning facilitator to create or at least enable these kinds of positive emotions.

Closely linked to positive emotions, and perhaps even indistinguishable from it is motivation. Given the vast literature on motivation and learning, it can probably safely be said that the two are indelibly intertwined, so we won't go into much detail here about the importance of motivation except where it relates to heutagogy. Motivation to learn has survival value and that is why we are naturally good at it. The organism's capacity to attend to relevant stimuli in the environment is the critical initial element in a process of analysis, decision-making and action. The human brain seeks to make patterns out of stimuli, to make sense of the environment, to find associations (e.g. Caine et al., 1999; Sousa, 2011). Moreover, the learner seeks to make even grander patterns with each new experience.

Associations are made by the learner, not by the teacher, no matter how hard teachers might try to make them on the learner's behalf. I like to ask groups to think of something that they learned once that really made a difference to their lives, either positively or negatively. My bet that the significant learning experience did not happen in the classroom is always won.

Motivation to learn is enhanced by: greater involvement in and control by the learner in the learning process; self-initiated learning; the opportunity to develop and share patterns; and relevance.

Ackoff and Greenberg (2008) provide a great example of the role of motivation in learning. This involved a group of students in a poor city neighbourhood with a high level of illiteracy and no interest in education (over 65% of households had no books). Knowing that these young people were incredibly street smart and not dumb a local university professor came up with a novel idea. He started to show old silent movies, which became very popular in a neighbourhood where entertainment was scarce. The interesting side-effect, however, was that the young people started teaching themselves how to read so that they could understand the captions.

Our environments

Finally, the other influence that has strongly affected the conceptualization of heutagogy has to do with how we understand context, the environment.

Humans have an apparently innate tendency to want to find simple explanations for phenomena and the essential reductionism that occurs in science supports this drive. Complexity theory (e.g. Lissack, 1999; Stacey et al., 2000; Waldrop, 1992) and systems thinking (Emery and Trist, 1965; Emery, 1993), however, claim that this can be counterproductive because the world in which we live is far more complex than can be explained by linear associations, or by simple cause and effect relationships. This is particularly true of social phenomena, which involve the interplay of rapidly changing, multiple variables that create a high level of unpredictability. The importance of complexity theory and systems thinking in relation to how we learn has been clearly described in a paper by Phelps et al. (2005). The key factors involved in these two theories can be summarized as (Hase, 2009, p. 46):

- systems are open and non-linear
- systems are affected by their environment (and vice-versa) in complex ways
- environment systems are not in equilibrium but are constantly adapting to changes
- these changes are unpredictable and non-linear but are self-generating and self-maintaining (autopoiesis)
- the system is greater than the sum of its parts, and hence, we cannot understand a system by only considering its parts
- outcomes are dependent on initial conditions that may be unknowable and, therefore, attempts at prediction are often futile (the butterfly effect)

- adaptation and then stability (bifurcation) occur as a result of stress on the system; big events may have small consequences and small events may have large consequences
- change is natural and evolutionary.

Thus, learning is an emergent process, unpredictable and involving the interplay of learner and context, both of which are in a state of constant flux (Doolittle, 2000). Learning outcomes are similarly unpredictable (Phelps et al., 2005) since learning is constructed by the learner in a process of purposeful, self-organized adaptation.

In summary, these lines of evidence suggest that we need to rethink how we engage people in so-called learning experiences. That is, we need to:

- involve the learner in designing their own learning content and process as a partner;
- make the curriculum flexible so that new questions and understanding can be explored as new neuronal pathways are developed;
- individualize learning as much as possible;
- provide flexible or negotiated assessment;
- enable the learner to contextualize concepts, knowledge and new understanding;
- provide lots of resources and let the learner explore;
- differentiate between knowledge and skill acquisition (competencies) and deep learning;
- recognize the importance of informal learning and that we only need to enable it rather than control it;
- have confidence in the learner; and
- recognize that teaching can become a block to learning.

We need to facilitate rather than teach, step back and guide, and provide a compass rather than a map.

Advances and applications

Since 2000, the study and use of heutagogical principles has steadily increased. For reasons that are not quite clear, a good deal of the discussion about heutagogy since its inception has concerned online learning (e.g. McNickle, 2003). Blaschke (2012) and Chapnick and Meloy (2005) conclude that web-based learning, new technologies and distance education methods lend themselves very well to a heutagogical approach.

Not everyone, however, has been enthusiastic about heutagogy (McAuliffe et al. 2008; McLoughlin and Lee, 2007). Critics suggest that organizations, like universities, that credential students would find flexible curricula and negotiated assessment, in particular, impractical. This is certainly true in the teacher-centred framework that currently exists in many educational institutions, particularly universities, where pedagogy is the dominant educational paradigm. Another, and more relevant concern (in our view) is the preparedness of the learner (Blaschke, 2012) to adopt what would be a completely different educational process. However, this need can be accommodated as Msilav and Setihako (2012) from the University of South Africa showed in using a heutagogical approach in an online teacher education module. They accommodated this important role of the teacher to nurture students until they can confidently take over their own learning.

Heutagogy, as described at the beginning of this chapter, deliberately challenges the prevailing educational paradigm. Despite some resistance, and having to negotiate learner preparedness, heutagogy has been applied, in a number of settings, including credentialing institutions with success.

The exciting notion of learner-generated contexts (LGC) (Luckin et al, 2005, 2011) fits neatly with the premises of heutagogy and, according to Whitworth (2008), the two have close ties. Mostly applied to web-based learning, LGC involves the learner actively finding learning resources rather than having them supplied by the teacher. Hence, the learner provides the context for the area being studied. This activity is undertaken with a goal in mind but changes the role of the learner from consumer to active participant in their own learning.

Ashton and Newman (2006) and Ashton and Elliott (2007) have applied a heutagogical approach to the design and delivery of a teacher education programme. The approach involved enabling learner-managed learning through flexible blended delivery. They found a number of positive effects that included: better teacher outcomes; increased capability among the student teachers; increased confidence; increased collaborative learning and peer learning processes; increased investigative capacity; and increased ability to question.

Canning and Callan (2010) in an observational study helped students in an early years education programme to 'discover their own strategies for learning, develop confidence through active participation and begin to share their knowledge and understanding of key concepts' (p. 74). They used reflective processes as a vehicle to achieve these outcomes. They found that the students increased control of their own learning, engaged in critical thinking in relation to theory and their own practice, improved their self-perception, became effective reflective practitioners both individually and collaboratively, and increased in confidence. Eberle and Childress (2009) using heutagogical principles have also found collaborative learning to lead to greater confidence among learners.

Similarly, Bhoyrub et al. (2010) believe that heutagogy provides a useful framework for creating confidence among nursing students for them to take advantage of learning opportunities in sometimes chaotic and highly complex clinical settings. It is up to the learners to make sense of their experience and to use their competencies in new and challenging situations that the workplace presents.

Albon (2006), within a heutaogical framework, had postgraduate education students develop assessment online and collaboratively. She found that the process drove learning further, increased students' autonomy and improved active learning. Albon also noted that the line between facilitator/guide and student became blurred as they learned together. Eberle and Childress (2009) also recommend the collaborative approach to designing assessment using double-loop learning.

The idea of flexible and negotiated assessment is not new and has existed for a number of years as a component of learning contracts (e.g. Anderson et al., 1998; Knowles, 1986). The learning contract provides an excellent vehicle for the negotiation of all aspects of the learning process, as long as it is in itself open to change as the learner's learning takes different turns.

Collaboration through teams or communities of practice is an important feature of heutagogy (Blaschke, 2012; Kenyon and Hase, 2010; Hase, 2009). Collaboration, however, is concerned with the learning process and learning to learn, as much as it is about finding content.

Conclusion

Deconstructing heutagogy reveals that there is nothing novel about its underpinnings, particularly the need to challenge prevailing dogma about the circumstances under which learners learn best. However, applying principles that can be sheeted back to heutagogy requires a major shift in the way in which we think about learning and education. Certainly heutagogy is a challenge to our credentialing institutions and the inflexibility that characterizes educational practice and teacher-centric learning. However, applications of heutagogy over the past 12 years or so have demonstrated that this challenge is one that can be taken up, and is resulting in some exciting innovation, particularly for learners.

References

Ackoff, R. L. and Greenberg, D. (2008), *Turning Learning Right Side Up: Putting Education Back on Track*. New Jersey: Pearson.

Albon, R. (2006), 'Motivation, dialogue, and heutagogy: driving collaborative assessment online', in J. R. Parker (ed.), *Proceedings of the Second IASTED International Conference on Education and Technology*. Calgary, AB: ACTA, 63–71.

Anderson, J. (2006), *The E-mature Learner*. Retrieved 29 November 2008 from: http://tre. ngfl.gov.uk/uploads/materials/24875/The_ema- ture_learner_John_Anderson.doc.

Anderson, G., Boud, D. and Sampson, J. (1998), 'Qualities of learning contracts', in J. Stephenson and M. Yorke (eds), *Capability and Quality in Higher Education*. London: Kogan Page, 162–73.

Argyris, C. and Schon, D. (1978), *Organizational Learning: A Theory of Action Perspective*. Reading, MA: Addison-Wesley.

Armstrong, J. S. (2012), *Natural Learning in Education. Encyclopedia of the Sciences of Learning*. Heidelberg: Springer.

Ashton, J. and Elliott, R. (2007), 'Juggling the balls – study, work, family and play: student perspectives on flexible and blended heutagogy. *European Early Childhood Education Research Journal*, 15(2), 167–81.

Ashton, J. and Newman, L. (2006), 'An unfinished symphony: 21st century teacher education using knowledge creating heutagogies', *British Journal of Educational Technology*, 37(6), 825–40.

Benfenati, F. (2007), 'Synaptic plasticity and the neurobiology of learning and memory', *Acta Biomed*, 78, 58–66.

Bhoyrub, J., Hurely, J., Neilson, G. R., Ramsay, M. and Smith, M. (2010), 'Heutagogy: an alternative practice based learning approach', *Nursing Education in Practice*, 10, 322–6.

Blaschke, L. M. (2012), 'Heutagogy and lifelong learning: a review of heutagogical practice and self-determined learning', *The International Review of Research in Open and Distance Learning*, 13(1). Retrieved 17 October 2012 from: www.irrodl.org/index.php/irrodl/article/view/1076/2087.

Bruner, J. (1960), *The Process of Education*. Cambridge, MA: Harvard University Press.

Caine, G., Nummela-Caine, R. and Crowell, S. (1999), *Mindshifts: A Brain-based Process for Restructuring Schools and Renewing Education* (2nd edn). Tucson, AZ: Zephyr Press.

Canning, N. (2010), 'Playing with heutagogy. Exploring strategies to empower mature learners in higher education', *Journal of Further and Higher Education*, 34(1), 59–71.

Canning, N. and Callan, S. (2010), 'Heutagogy: spirals of reflection to empower learners in higher education', *Reflective Practice*, 11(1), 71–82.

Chapnick, S. and Meloy, J. (2005), *Renaissance E-learning: Creating Dramatic and Unconventional Learning Experiences*. San Francisco, CA: Pfeiffer.

Coomey, M. and Stephenson, J. (2001), 'Online learning: it is all about dialogue, involvement, support and control – according to the research', in J. Stephenson (ed.), *Teaching and Learning Online: Pedagogies for New Technologies*. London: Kogan Page, 37–52.

Coughlan, R. (2004), 'From the challenge to the response', *Proceedings of the BiTE Project Conference*. Adastral Park, December.

Craik, F. I. M. and Tulving, E. (1975), 'Depth of processing and the retention of words in episodic memory', *Journal of Experimental Psychology General*, 104, 268–94.

Damasio, A. (2003), *Looking for Spinoza: Joy, Sorrow, and the Feeling Brain*. London: William Heinemann.

Davis, B., Sumara, D. and Luce-Kapler, R. (2000), *Engaging Minds: Learning and Teaching in a Complex World*. Mahwah: Lawrence Erlbaum.

Dewey, J. (1938), *Experience and Education*. New York: Macmillan.

Doidge, N. (2007), *The Brain that Changes Itself: Stories of Personal Triumph from the Frontiers of Brain Science*. New York: Viking.

Dolcos, F., Labar, K. S. and Cabeza, R. (2004), 'Interaction between the amygdala and the medial temporal lobe memory system predicts better memory for emotional events', *Neuron*, 42, 855–63.

Doll, W. E. (1989), *A Post-modern Perspective on Curriculum*. New York: New York Teachers College.

Doolittle, P. E. (2000), *Complex Constructivism: A Theoretical Model of Complexity and Cognition*. Retrieved 28 August 2012 from: www.tandl.vt.edu/doolittle/research/complex1.html.

Eberle, J. and Childress, M. (2009), 'Using heutagogy to address the needs of online learners'. in P. Rogers, G. A. Berg, J. V. Boettecher and L. Justice (eds), *Encyclopedia of Distance Learning* (2nd edn). New York: Idea Group Inc, 181–7.

Emery, M. (1993), *Participative Design for Participative Democracy* (2nd edn). Canberra, Australia: Centre for Continuing Education, The Australian National University.

Emery, F. E. and Trist, E. L. (1965), 'The causal texture of organizational environments', *Human Relations*, 18(1), 21–32.

Freire, P. (1972), *Pedagogy of the Oppressed*. Harmondsworth, UK: Penguin.

—. (1995), *Pedagogy of Hope. Reliving Pedagogy of the Oppressed*. New York: Continuum

Gabrieli J. D .E, Desmond J. E, Demb J. B, Wagner, A. D, Stone M. V, and Vaidya C. J. (1996), 'Functional magnetic resonance imaging of semantic memory processes in the frontal lobes', *Psychological Science*, 7, 278–83.

Gopnik, A., Meltzoff, A. N. and Kuhl, P. K. (2000), *The Scientist in the Crib*. New York: William Morrow.

Grant, H. M., Bredahl, L. C., Clay, J., Ferrie, J., Groves, J. E., McDorman, T. A. and Dark, V. J. (1998), 'Context-dependent memory of meaningful material: information for students', *Applied Cognitive Psychology,* 12, 617–23.

Graves, N. (ed) (1993), *Learner Managed Learning: Practice, Theory and Policy.* Leeds: WEF and HEC.

Hase, S. (2002), 'Simplicity in complexity: capable people and capable organisations need each other'. Paper presented at the *Australian Vocational Education and Training Research Association (AVETRA) Conference*, Melbourne, 22–24 April. Retrieved 2 July 2012 from: http://epubs.scu.edu.au/cgi/viewcontent.cgi?article=1145&context=gcm_pubs.

—. (2009), 'Heutagogy and e-learning in the workplace: some challenges and opportunities'*, Impact: Journal of Applied Research in Workplace E-learning,* 1(1), 43–52.

Hase, S. and Kenyon, C. (2000), 'From andragogy to heutagogy', *ultiBASE*, 5(3). Retrieved 23 October 2012 from: http://ultibase.rmit.edu.au/Articles/dec00/hase1.pdf.

—. (2003), 'Heutagogy and developing capable people and capable workplaces: strategies for dealing with complexity'. *Proceedings of The Changing Face of Work and Learning Conference.* Edmonton, AB: University of Alberta. Retrieved 23 October 2012 from: www.wln.ualberta.ca/papers/pdf/17.pdf.

—. (2007), 'Heutagogy: a child of complexity theory', *Complicity*, 4(1). Retrieved 23 October 2012 from: www.complexityandeducation.ualberta.ca/COMPLICITY4/documents/ Complicity_41k_HaseKenyon.pdf.

—. (2010), 'Learner defined curriculum: Heutagogy and action learning in vocational training', *Southern Institute of Technology Journal of Applied Research*, Special Edition on Action Research. Retrieved from: http://sitjar.sit.ac.nz.

Hasher, L. and Zacks, R. T. (1984), 'Automatic and effortful processes in Memory', *Journal of Experimental Psychology General,* 198, 356–88.

Ingleton, J. (1999), 'Emotion in learning: a neglected dynamic'. Paper presented at the *Higher Education Research and Development Society of Australasia (HERDSA) Annual International Conference*, Melbourne, Australia, 12–15 July. Retrieved 23 October 2012 from: www.herdsa.org.au/wp-content/uploads/conference/1999/pdf/Ingleton.PDF.

Johnstone, A. H. and Percival, F. (1976), 'Attention breaks in lectures', *Education in Chemistry*, 13 (3), 49–50.

Kenyon, C and Hase, S. (2010), 'Andragogy and heutagogy in postgraduate work', in T. Kerry (ed.), *Meeting the Challenges of Change in Postgraduate Higher Education.* London: Continuum Press, 165–77.

Khaneman, D. (2011), *Thinking Fast and Slow.* London: Penguin.

Knowles, M. S. (1980), *Modern Practice of Adult Education: Andragogy versus Pedagogy.* Chicago: Association Press/Follett.

—. (1986), *Using Learning Contracts.* San Francisco, CA: Jossey-Bass.

LeDoux, J. (2002), *Synaptic Self: How Our Brains Become Who We Are*. New York: Viking Press.

Lissack, M. R. (1999), 'Complexity: the science, its vocabulary and its relation to organizations', *Emergence*, 1(1), 110–26.

Long, D. (1990), *Learner Managed Learning: The Key to Life Long Learning and Development*. New York: Kogan Page.

Luckin, R., du Boulay, B., Smith, H., Underwood, J., Fitzpatrick, G., Holmberg, J., Kerawalla, L., Tunley, H., Brewster, D. and Pearce, D. (2005), 'Using mobile technology to create flexible learning contexts', *Journal of Interactive Media in Education*, 22, 1–21.

Luckin, R., Clark, W., Garnett, F. Whitworth, A., Akass, J., Cook, J., Day, P., Ecclesfield, N., Hamilton, T. and Robertson, J. (2011), 'Learner generated contexts: a framework to support the effective use of technology for learning', in M. J. W. Lee and C. McLoughlin (eds), *Web 2.0-based E-learning: Applying Social Informatics in Tertiary Teaching*. Hershey: Information Science Reference, 70–84.

McAuliffe, M. B., Hargreaves, D. J., Winter, A. J. and Chadwick, G. (2008), 'Does pedagogy still rule?' Paper presented at the *19th Annual Conference of Australasian Association for Engineer Education*, 7–10 December, Central Queensland University, Yeppoon.

McLoughlin, C. and Lee, M. J. W. (2007), 'Social software and participatory learning: pedagogical choices with technology affordances in the Web 2.0 era'. *Proceedings of the Ascilite Conference*, Singapore, 2–5 December. Retrieved 23 October 2012 from: www.ascilite.org.au/conferences/singapore07/procs/mcloughlin.pdf.

McNickle, C. (2003), 'The impact that ICT has on how we learn – pedagogy, andragogy or heutagogy?' *Proceedings of the Sustaining Quality Learning Environments: 16th ODLAA Biennial Forum Conference*. Canberra: Canberra Institute of Technology.

Medina, J. (2008a), *Brain Rules*. Seattle: Pear Press.

—. (2008b), 'Why emotional memories are unforgettable', *Psychiatric Times*, 14–17.

Merriam, S. B., Caffarella, R. and Baumgartner, L. (2007). *Learning in Adulthood: A Comprehensive Guide* (3rd edn). New York: Wiley.

Middendorf, J. and A. Kalish (1996), 'The "change-up" in lectures', *National Teaching and Learning Forum*, 2 (5). Retrieved June 4, 2013, from http://www.ntlf.com/html/pi/9601/article1.htm.

Msilav, V. and Setihako, A. (2012), 'Teaching still matters: experiences on developing a heutagogical online module at UNISA', *Journal of Educational and Social Research*, 2(2), 65–71.

Phelps, R., Hase, S. and Ellis, A. (2005), 'Competency, capability, complexity and computers: exploring a new model for conceptualising end-user computer education', *British Journal of Educational Technology*, 36(1), 67–85.

Piaget, J. (1973), *To Understand is to Invent*. New York: Grossman.

Rogers, C. (1969), *Freedom to Learn: A View of What Education Might Become*. Columbus, OH: Charles Merill.

Rosenzweig, M. R., Krech, D., Bennett, E. L. and Diamond, M. C. (1962), 'Effects of environmental complexity and training on brain chemistry and anatomy: a replication and extension', *Journal of Comparative and Physiological Psychology*, 55, 429–37.

Sousa, D. (2011), *How the Brain Learns*. Thousand Oaks, CA: Corwin Press.

Stacey, R. D., Griffin, D. and Shaw, P. (2000), *Complexity and Management: Fad or Radical Challenge to Systems Thinking?* London: Routledge.

Stephenson, J. (1996), 'Beyond competence to capability and the learning society', *Capability*, 2(1), 60–2.

Stephenson, J. and Weil, S. (1992), *Quality in Learning: A Capability Approach in Higher Education*. London: Kogan Page.

Sumara, D. J. and Davis, B. (1997), 'Enactivist theory and community learning: toward a complexified understanding of action research. Educational', *Action Research*, 5(3), 403–22.

Tay, B. H. and Hase, S. (2004), 'The role of action research in workplace PhDs', *Action Learning and Action Research Journal*, 9(1), 81–92.

Vygotsky, L. S. (1978), *Mind in Society: The Development of Higher Psychological Processes*. Cambridge, MA: Harvard University Press.

Waldrop, M. (1992), *Complexity: The Emerging Science at the Edge of Order and Chaos*. London: Penguin.

Whitworth, A. (2008), 'Learner generated contexts: critical theory and ICT education'. Paper presented at the *6th Panhellenic Conference on Information and Communication Technologies in Education*, Limassol, Cyprus, 25–28 September.

Willis, J. (2006), *Research-based Strategies to Ignite Student Learning: Insights from a Neurologist and Classroom Teacher*. Alexandria, VA: ASCD.

Part Two

Applying Heutagogy in
Formal Education

3

Crafting Learner-Centred Processes Using Action Research and Action Learning

Bob Dick

Summary

Almost all adults are capable of taking control of their learning. Often, though, they carry expectations from previous experiences that get in the way. Self-directed learning doesn't always just happen. Sometimes it has to be crafted. Fortunately, participant expectations can be negotiated, goals can be clarified and a sense of community can be built within the classroom or change team. When that is done, the result is more likely to be a strongly learner-centred and learner-directed situation. Strong engagement and deep learning can then ensue. This chapter explains how it can be done, illustrating the approach with examples from university classes and action learning teams.

Introduction

The following account is based on several decades of experience in setting up learner-directed experiences. The main emphasis is on participatory university classes and participant-driven action learning programmes. I also draw less directly on my experience of facilitating public workshops for skills development, and in other community and organizational change programmes, though I don't describe them here. In almost all of this work, small teams provided the immediate context for individual actions and learning.

To preview the details that follow, the early stages of these learning or change experiences are important in setting the scene. At these times I give particular attention to six aspects of class or team functioning:

- clarifying those outcomes that are mandated elsewhere, and negotiating those outcomes where there is choice
- building a sense of community in larger groups and establishing strong and supportive relationships in small groups
- reaching agreement on my role and the roles of other participants
- negotiating the processes to be used when we and they meet
- identifying any people not present who are to be involved or kept informed in any way
- relating the activity to the personal goals or interests of participants, especially what they hope to learn from engagement in the activity.

It seems that every class or change programme is unique. Therefore, the form taken by these early activities varies from situation to situation. Below I first describe setting up a typical learner-centred university class that can serve as an exemplar. I follow this with one example of the initiation of an action learning programme for organizational change. From these two instances I then draw the relevant principles of support for learner-directed learning.

A learner-directed university class

It will be seen that much of what I describe below is consistent with the literature on adult learning from such authors as Malcolm Knowles (1972) and Stephen Brookfield (1990), for example. Though I later consulted those literatures, my initial ideas were drawn more from industrial democracy and employee participation, and from the work redesign championed by Fred Emery and Merrelyn Emery (1975). From the beginning my aim was to establish classes in which class participants, within certain necessary but minimal constraints, decided the class content and the learning processes used, and then co-managed the resulting class with me.

This did not happen as easily or as quickly as I expected. When I first invited class members in the beginning week of the class to join me in this endeavour they responded with anxiety rather than the enthusiasm I had anticipated. I later found that Trevor Williams (1972) experienced a very similar reaction to his attempt to increase classroom democracy. Perhaps this explains why other academics I met abandoned their attempts to introduce classroom democracy (see Dick, 1992). Williams and I both persisted and were eventually pleased with the results we obtained.

However, it did take some years of trial and error before I was satisfied with the results. It happened only when I used the early weeks of the classes to prepare the class members for a more self-directed role. I also found that most class members favoured an approach that already had some pre-existing structure. They found being confronted with a blank slate too stressful.

In a typical semester at the time I was responsible for six or seven different classes. This allowed me to experiment with multiple approaches. By the time I had been a full-time academic for less than a decade, the approaches that led most consistently to success had emerged. I was also able to draw on consulting work outside the university, where I made use of many of the approaches developed in the classroom.

As each class was different, I'll use as an example a year-long honours-level course in 'Advanced social consultancy' to illustrate many of the features that I learned to incorporate into my classroom work. As it was independently evaluated (Johnston, 1984) I also have some assurance that participants thought very well of it both during the class and in the light of their subsequent work experience after graduation.

A substantial part of this course consisted of experiential workshops. Most of these were designed, facilitated and evaluated by small groups of class members. Their class colleagues were their participants. However, this happened only after I had facilitated the early weeks to create a sufficiently supportive environment and appropriate expectations of me and of the course.

The main thrust of those early weeks of the class was fourfold. First, I did what I could to alleviate anxieties originating from previous experience, especially about assessment and small group work. Second, I explained the 'default' structure that would provide a starting point for our negotiation. Third, there were activities to help class members to relate the course, its content and its approach to their life and career. Fourth, most activities were done in a way that modelled and built a collaborative environment characterized by strong and supportive relationships. The next section provides some more detailed examples.

Crafting the context

The following incomplete list will illustrate some of the activities that contributed to the creation of a class atmosphere that supported self-directed learning.

Formation of 'home groups'. The class varied in size from year to year within a range of 12 to 30, or occasionally a few more. It seemed desirable for participants to also be able to relate to a smaller group of their colleagues. Therefore, in the second week or thereabouts, participants organized themselves into groups of about three or four participants by self-selection. Many (though not all) class activities were then performed in or by these groups.

Community and relationship building. Every week for the first few weeks we spent time in the whole class in activities where we learned more about each other. In addition, intense relationship building was done in the home groups. The home group activities were designed for people to experience each other as real and complex beings, not as 'students' – a term I deliberately avoided. Many of the other activities in the early weeks were also done in ways that improved relationships. About half of the activities were in home groups while in the other half the group membership was deliberately changed. My aim was that by week 5, everybody would have had close interaction with everyone else in the course.

Meeting with the previous cohort. I had reason to believe that in the early weeks of the class, many participants assumed that my allegiance was to the university and to academia rather than to them. This perception, coupled with their expectations from other classes, initially coloured their perceptions of what I said, often substantially. Therefore, on a weekend very early in the course, class participants from the present and the previous cohort met informally at my home. I provided refreshments and facilitated a round of introductions. To make it easy for people to talk openly I then left the room.

Contact with practitioners. I desired to provide participants with information about the relevance of the work to their later career. An early activity was therefore adopted to put them in contact with practitioners in the field of community and organizational change. Four or five practitioners, chosen to be a diverse selection, spent half a day with the class. In small groups to allow deep interaction they talked about what practice was like and what skills and understanding it required. Over the course of the session each class participant interacted with all of the visiting practitioners. In later weeks, these practitioners and others met semi-regularly with pairs or trios of class participants to continue the discussion.

Life and career planning. An early aim in the course was to help participants choose learning goals that were personally relevant. In most years this was addressed partly through a life and career planning activity. Participants attempted to anticipate what their future life and career might be like. They were then encouraged to identify the relevant skills and understanding that could be acquired in the class.

Workshop on experiential learning. An important aim of the course was to integrate theory and practice. One vehicle for achieving this is experiential learning as described by David Kolb (1984). I knew that many experienced trainers and educators would find it challenging to design and facilitate an experiential activity. I therefore facilitated an experiential workshop on experiential workshops. Class participants took part in the workshop. In the latter stages of the workshop they deduced from their experience the principles and processes they could use to design and conduct their own workshops.

Course design. Finally, by week 4 or 5, I judged that the climate was sufficiently supportive for participants to be willing to respond to challenge and responsibility. Drawing on what we had learned and decided in the earlier weeks, collectively we designed the first semester of the course. We began by agreeing on the topics we would try to cover during the course. With this as background we identified the types of learning activity that would allow us to address these topics in a way that integrated theory and practice. Finally, each home group volunteered some topics drawn from our collective list that they were prepared to help the class learn.

By the time this design evolved it worked well. It made sense, and was not difficult to do. I sometimes wondered why I had not had the understanding to incorporate these and similar activities into the class from the beginning. The ease arose partly because, within the classroom, we were largely in control of our own destiny. Other aspects of design and conduct were less in our control and therefore more problematic. Some aspects of self-direction by the participants were unavoidably constrained by external requirements, as they so often are.

Assessment was a particular difficulty. For instance, if no external constraints existed I would not have graded the course. Class participants enthusiastically proposed activities that didn't contribute to their grades, demonstrating that learning and enjoyment were sufficient motivators for them. However, an ungraded course was not an available choice. A description of the process adopted for negotiating the assessment illustrates the self-direction that was achieved despite the constraints. It also illustrates some of the action research principles that allowed the class to continue to improve from year to year.

Negotiating assessment

Assessment was explained and negotiated using a 'standard assessment package', which offered several advantages. The standard package was based on the assessment used by the previous cohort and then modified by that cohort during their final participative evaluation of their class. I explained to the present cohort that this was intended as a starting point for negotiation.

There were limits to negotiability. To maintain equity between courses, in theory only the academic department in which I worked could approve assessment. To some extent this was true. However, provided there were no surprises for the department I found I was able to modify the assessment within limits. My undertaking to the department at the beginning of the year was that I would maintain assessment that was equitable and 'true to label' – relevant to the stated course subject matter. My commitment to class members was that I would accept *any* modification that did not distort the proclaimed aims of the course and that was fair to other classes, to all class participants and to me.

Negotiation of the assessment was conducted in three phases. Initially the class as a whole could propose changes. Subject to the conditions already mentioned these were accepted. In practice, proposals from the class were reasonable and constructive almost without exception. The assessment as modified could be further renegotiated by any small group within the class, again subject to the same conditions as before. Finally, any individual participant could further renegotiate the assessment. Further, to provide a 'safety net' for those who later found that their ambitions overreached their abilities, any class participant could negotiate to revert to the standard assessment package.

From the description above you will have noted that each cohort was able to negotiate the assessment (collectively and individually) at the beginning of the year. In addition they could propose amendments to the standard assessment package at the end of the year in the form of suggestions to the next cohort. The negotiated assessment available to each group and participant further allowed that assessment to be tailored to individual needs. The standard package was thus enhanced from year to year to become an improving record of how assessment might be done. The guiding principles were those of action research, which was also applied to evaluate and improve other aspects of the course.

Evaluation strategies for ongoing improvement

Participatory evaluation contributed in important ways to the evolving design of the course. The evaluation of the assessment (described above) took place at the end of the course year. It was accompanied by an extensive evaluation of other aspects of the course. A mid-course evaluation was conducted after first semester, feeding into a participative course redesign at the start of the second semester. Brief evaluations were scheduled at other times to take stock of how we were going. Other course activities were separately evaluated. I describe two of the important evaluation components below.

The *end-of-course evaluation* served several purposes. As a reflective activity on the class as a whole it reinforced what participants had learned. It refined the standard assessment package, as previously mentioned. It provided me with feedback about what was working and where there was most room for improvement. As will become evident, it also allowed one cohort's learning to be communicated to the next cohort.

To assist participants to put aside their participant roles and adopt the role of evaluators, this final evaluation was done off-campus. It took place in the final week of the course. We first recalled the overall design of the course and its week-by-week components. As we did so we identified strengths and weaknesses. We did this, first individually and then in small groups, to give all participants the chance to contribute. As a final step, participants agreed on two lists of suggestions: to me, about how I might further improve the course; and to the next cohort, about how they might gain the most from the course for themselves. I communicated both sets of suggestions to the next cohort at the start of the next course.

Every *class activity was evaluated* by those presenting it, involving others when appropriate. Foremost among the multiple aims was to encourage participants to regard reflection and evaluation as an integral part of everything that they did. In participative activities such as workshops it provided feedback from participants (the 'audience') to those presenting it. For all activities it provided me with information about the depths of understanding achieved by class members.

Participative evaluation was included in the design of each of the experiential workshops facilitated by class groups or by me. Each written assignment was accompanied by the author's own evaluation of its strengths and weaknesses, and a statement of what the author learned by doing the assignment. Small groups were involved in off-campus field projects, and we set aside class time in which these groups could report on and evaluate their progress and learning.

In *all* evaluation I tried to be non-judgemental in my own feedback. I provided my feedback in the form of commendation for strengths, and suggestions for improvement. In participative evaluations I did what I could to encourage a non-judgemental climate. My intention was that all evaluation was primarily a source of learning. I also hoped that it would help class members view the assessment of the course as merely one component of the course, not as the main outcome. There is evidence that this was to some extent achieved – most participants voluntarily committed time and effort to course activities that did not have an assessment component.

There was much more to this class than I've described above, and even more if I take into account the many other classes informed by a similar philosophy. However, the details I've provided do sufficiently identify the main ways in which a context was developed in support of self-directed learning. It will be seen that action learning teams as described below, though different in detail, share much of the same philosophy.

Action learning

Action learning is also an experiential educational process. Small groups of participants meet regularly or semi-regularly to help each other plan their activities and learn from their experience. In its original form developed by Reg Revans (1982), groups of senior managers (often CEOs) from different organizations brought individual projects and problems to their meetings. Since then many varied forms of action learning have arisen, as Judy O'Neil and Victoria Marsick (2007) document. In particular, it's now common for a team within a single organization to be set up to work on a single project. The approach I describe below follows this pattern. I've used similar approaches in community development, and colleagues and I have also applied action learning and action research to an offshore PhD programme (Sankaran et al., 2006).

Here I limit my description to those aspects of my approach that are most illustrative of ways of creating a supportive context for self-directed learning. A more complete description is available on the web (Dick, 2011).

In one respect I observe a practice followed by Revans though since mostly abandoned by other writers, as Pedler and Abbott (2008) have explained. I provide only *initial* facilitation. I encourage action learning team members to take over the facilitation as soon as they are willing to do so. Some preparation in the organization itself is helpful. As with the university class described earlier my intention is for the team to become self-directed. And as with those classes, some initial activities are required for that to happen. I provide more detail in the following paragraphs.

Creating a supportive organizational context

Organizational teams frequently have less autonomy than university classes. Too easily, the organization intrudes on the operation of the teams. I have found a number of practices that appear to increase the effectiveness of the teams, both in terms of their successful completion of their task, and their development of useful skills and understanding. Most importantly, these have usually included:

- having sufficient senior management support that teams are adequately resourced, including enough time to accomplish the task
- choosing tasks that are complex enough to present a challenge for the teams while being contained enough to be completed in about three months
- having small teams consisting entirely of participants who have volunteered for those teams and are enthusiastic about the team's task
- providing teams with access to coaching, mentoring or other forms of skills development, and (if required) political advice.

Some of these warrant further comment.

Choice of projects has proved to be important. More relevant learning is achieved when projects are complex enough to require initial planning followed by some adjustment of the plans through trial and error. In addition it is important that the projects are real, carrying real responsibility. Otherwise the team members' enthusiasms are less likely to be engaged, and organizational or community resources are less likely to be provided.

To further engage project team members it is important that the team has genuine autonomy. The organization or community will probably specify desired project outcomes and constraints on available resources. Within these limits it is usually possible (and advisable) that the team manages the planning and implementation of the project with minimal oversight.

As Paul Gorrell and John Hoover (2009) report, coaching and action learning complement each other in valuable ways. Coaching allows team members to obtain from outside the team the skills and understanding they may require to facilitate the team process. In much of the action learning described in the literature, teams have access to a sponsor who has influence, and a mentor who can offer political advice. I've found these useful.

According to Pedler et al. (2005) it is also increasingly common for action learning programmes to provide skill development and relevant information to action learning team members. This has been my experience too. I provide the skill development in the form of workshops if and when participants request it.

Setting up the action learning teams

In setting up an action learning team, my usual practice is to encourage team members to become self-managing as soon as they are willing. When roles and responsibilities have been suitably negotiated with the organization or community, three meetings with each team are usually enough to achieve team self-management. In a first meeting of three hours or a little more, I facilitate. Subsequent meetings are briefer, usually between an hour and an hour and a half. The second meeting is usually facilitated by a team member who has volunteered to do so. I act as a supportive coach to that person. At a third meeting I am usually present, but intervene little or not at all. My purpose is to demonstrate to participants that they are capable of managing their own team dynamics and their own learning. More details of the three meetings follow.

As mentioned, I facilitate the first meeting. In the time available, I accomplish as many as possible of the following tasks:

- We build supportive and collaborative relationships between team members. The team members exchange information that reveals each of them as a complex and real individual. For example, if they are willing, this might be done by describing 'turning points' in their life and work – people and events that made a difference for them. My assumption is that when people experience each other as real, their commitment to each other and their willingness to collaborate is enhanced.

- We clarify the team project in outcome terms. We do this by identifying how the team will know that they have successfully completed the planning and implementation of their project.

- We identify the 'stakeholders': the other people who have a stake in the team project. Time permitting, we may also give time to planning the extent of their involvement and how it will be achieved. Alternatively, the team can address this at their second meeting.

- We undergo an activity that sensitizes the team members to the dynamics of their interaction. Team members draw on their previous experience of teams and groups that were effective and enjoyable, and those that were not. The outcome of the activity is a very small list of 'process guidelines' that team members agree they would like to follow as they work together. They revisit these guidelines during a review phase of each meeting.

- Team members identify the individual skills and understanding that each of them plans to achieve by working on the action learning project. Each of them is encouraged to choose learning goals that will be appropriate for the organization or community and also relevant for each of them individually.

At the end of this first meeting we use the process guidelines (fourth bullet point above) to evaluate how well the meeting worked. In addition, one of the team members volunteers to facilitate the next meeting. Of the activities we do, the relationship building is both most time-consuming and most important. The deeper the relationships developed, the sooner the team takes control of its own process and project and learning.

At the second meeting a team member facilitates. The team addresses any incomplete issues left over from the first meeting, and begins to plan how it will approach the project. More often than not, it decides the level of involvement appropriate for each stakeholder, and how this will be achieved. We arrange that throughout this second meeting any team member (including the facilitator) can call 'time out' at any time. If this occurs we pause the process and analyse what is happening. I provide supportive coaching to the facilitator or other team members when it appears desirable, though in general I try to minimize my interventions. The meeting concludes, as before, with an evaluation.

Third and subsequent meetings begin with a report from participants about what has happened between meetings. Each meeting then develops project action plans further, and ends with an evaluation. Team members rotate facilitation of meetings between them, so that each of them is developing skills in project and change management, and in facilitative leadership.

Between meetings, team members carry out any actions that have been planned at the previous meeting. In addition, the facilitators of the previous session and the next session meet to reflect on what was done and what will be done.

Drawing lessons from the examples

There are patterns evident in the descriptions I have so far provided. In retrospect, I could relate these to a variety of literatures – as, indeed, most applied endeavours involving collective and individual human behaviour can be. In reality, though, I have largely avoided directly relevant literature when I have been initiating and refining my professional practice. Although I may have reinvented the wheel, it has been a fine way to really understand the wheel. My strategy has been to approach the literature only after thoughtful trial and error has already provided me with satisfying outcomes. The literature then provides further refinement. Other authors such as Stewart Hase and Chris Kenyon (2000, 2007) have identified many of the varied literatures that are relevant to learner-directed learning. Accordingly, what follows is a brief account of the aspects of activities that experience has taught me to heed in the classroom, the workshop venue and in change programmes generally.

When I reflect on the way in which my experience has guided me towards my current practices, three emphases stand out. I pay more attention to relationships than it is my natural inclination to do so. After sometimes-painful trial and error I have found ways of offering participants genuine autonomy by learning what boundaries to build around their freedom. Experience has impressed upon me the importance to people of having experiences and responsibilities that are meaningful for *them*.

Discovering the importance of relationships was the hardest lesson. By nature I'm reticent, and more of a theorist than a practitioner. But perhaps that was a good starting position. My own tendency to cringe at the thought of some activities I experienced as a participant motivated me to find alternatives.

Thus impelled, I searched out or developed processes that combined high levels of self-disclosure with instructions and invitations that legitimized the activity for participants and increased safety for them. I learned to offer participants choice so that they could match the chosen activity to the level of safety they required. The effort was repaid. The more successful the relationship building, the more effective the following activities were for the participants and for myself.

It's tempting to assume that one either instructs people what to do or offers them autonomy – to be an autocrat or a democrat. In practice it has worked better for me to aim for a resolution of the tension between those alternatives. In my earliest classroom work I erred on the side of offering too much autonomy and too much challenge. Stephen Brookfield (2010, p. 5), one of the early champions for democratic education, described democratic leadership as a 'relative rarity'. He goes on to say that this arises from an 'unwillingness . . . to trust people to know what's best for them'. As mentioned earlier, many educators who pursue democracy in the classroom abandon the attempt for lack of success – and sometimes, I suspect, from an unwillingness to trust.

The design principle implied by my early experience was to offer freedom within limits. Results were then further enhanced when the limits were both clear and jointly negotiable. When the boundaries were clear and fully discussable, participants in the classroom and elsewhere more willingly took on the responsibilities that autonomy required. Initially it was still often a struggle. Later the negotiations about the task and responsibilities and limits became much easier and more effective when trusting relationships had already been established.

It may be relevant here to note a trend towards providing facilitation for action learning teams, as Mike Pedler and Christine Abbott (2008) report.

My assumption has been that skills and understanding are enhanced when participants accept responsibility for their own learning. Teachers don't teach, I have long believed. Learners learn. 'Teachers' (the quotes are deliberate) provide a context within which learning is encouraged and enabled.

The growth of facilitated action learning teams is most probably driven by the experience of other facilitators. I assume they do it because it worked for them. It is contrary to Revans' usual practice and recommendations. I think it was my emphasis on relationships that allowed me to achieve good results from minimal facilitation. My experience therefore drew me in a different direction.

Finally, there is the choice of the projects and activities and responsibilities that participants are being invited to embrace. Are they seen as worth the time and effort they consume? Finding goals that are beneficial for the participant is part of this, so some elements of individual choice are important. If the goals are also beneficial for the wider community or organization then that can further increase the perceived worth.

Again I found that strong relationships provided a foundation for this. When people identify with the larger systems – the class, the action learning team, the community or organization – the contributions to those systems are more valued. At the same time, the closeness of relationships within the team offers a source of support to the individuals. Such support encourages participants more willingly to take on the responsibilities.

My design principle has become: freedom within clear and negotiable limits, high challenge and high support within and beyond the team or group.

Conclusion

It seems to me that each of us is capable of adopting many different roles and exhibiting many different behaviours. We have within us many different capacities, some of them conflicting. For example, I believe we are born with capacities for both competition and collaboration, and for exhibiting these in both constructive and destructive forms. Our perception of a situation triggers a selection of roles and behaviours.

When I set up an action learning team or initiate a class or experiential workshop or change programme, I assume that my responsibility is to create an environment that will elicit constructive behaviours and roles. If the goal is a learner-centred activity, I need to find a way of creating an environment that will engender and support learner-centred attitudes and behaviour. If participants' initial expectations do not match that goal, then somehow I must first address that. Because people differ, this will not always be simple. Multiple triggers may be required to elicit the appropriate behaviour. Often some trial and error will be required before the appropriate roles are activated.

Fortunately, there have been some nearly universal aspects identified in the learner-centred activities I've initiated. As illustrated by the examples I've described above, three in particular have been apparent: challenge, autonomy and support. In these examples I've aimed at creating a challenging, achievable and worthwhile task, providing participants with as much autonomy as possible, and engendering support based on strong and collaborative relationships. When I've succeeded in achieving this, participants have usually risen to the occasion, often surprising themselves and others with their learning and their achievements.

References

Brookfield, S. D. (1990), *The Skillful Teacher: On Technique, Trust, and Responsiveness in the Classroom*. San Francisco, CA: Jossey Bass.

—. (2010), 'Leading democratically', *New Directions for Adult and Continuing Education*, 128, 5–13.

Dick, B. (1992), 'Democracy for learners', in B. Smith (ed.), *Management Development in Australia*. Sydney: Harcourt Brace Jovanovich, 140–8.

—. (2011), '*Action Learning: Using Project Teams to Build Leadership and Resilience*', Interchange, online. Retrieved 28 November 2012 from: www.aral.com.au/resources/actionlearning.pdf.

Emery, F. E. and Emery, M. (1975), *Participative Design: Work and Community Life*. Canberra, ACT: Centre for Continuing Education, Australian National University.

Gorrell, P. J. and Hoover, J. (2009), *The Coaching Connection: A Manager's Guide to Developing Individual Potential in the Context of the Organization*. New York: Amacom.

Hase, S. and Kenyon, C. (2000), 'From andragogy to heutagogy', *Ultibase*, RMIT. Retrieved 28 November 2012 from http://ultibase.rmit.edu.au/Articles/dec00/hase2.htm.

—. (2007), 'Heutagogy: a child of complexity theory', *Complicity*, 4(1), 111–18.

Johnston, D. A. (1984). '*Psychology in the 1980s: An Ongoing Search for an Education and a Career: The Experience of Recent Fourth Year Psychology Graduates of the University of Queensland*'. Unpublished honours thesis. St Lucia: Department of Psychology, University of Queensland.

Knowles, M. S. (1972), *The Modern Practice of Adult Education*. Chicago, IL: Associated Press.

Kolb, D. A. (1984), *Experiential Learning: Experience as the Source of Learning and Development*. Englewood Cliffs, NJ: Prentice-Hall.

O'Neil, J. and Marsick, V. J. (2007), *Understanding Action Learning: Theory into Practice*. New York: Amacom.

Pedler, M. and Abbott, C. (2008), 'Am I doing it right? Facilitating action learning for service improvement', *Leadership in Health Services*, 21(3), 185–99.

Pedler, M., Burgoyne, J. and Brook, C. (2005), 'What has action learning learned to become?' *Action Learning: Research and Practice*, 2(1), 49–68.

Revans, R. W. (1982), *The Origins and Growth of Action Learning*. Bromley, UK: Chartwell-Bratt.

Sankaran, S., Hase, S., Dick, B. and Davies, A. (2006), 'Reflections on developing an offshore, action research/learning-based Ph.D. program', *Action Learning: Research and Practice*, 3(2), 197–211.

Williams, T. (1972), *Democracy in Learning*. Canberra, ACT: Centre for Continuing Education, Australian National University.

4

E-Learning and Self-Determined Learning Skills

Lisa Marie Blaschke

Summary

This chapter will examine the role that Web 2.0 technology can play in supporting a heutagogical approach to teaching and learning. It considers the key features of the technology that support this approach, such as the freedom to discover and create one's own content, to collaborate and build communities of learning, to reflect on what is learned and how it is learned and to determine one's own learning paths. In addition, the chapter will provide guidelines for instructors on incorporating a heutagogical teaching approach into their courses using Web 2.0 tools. Practical examples for application in the classroom are provided.

Introduction

At the time that Stewart Hase and Chris Kenyon (2000) first introduced the concept of heutagogy, technology and education were not sufficiently well aligned to fully support a self-determined approach to learning. Just over a decade a later, it is a different story. Enter the age of open education resources, edupunks, social media, massive open online courses (MOOCs) and digital badges – the start of an era where learners have substantially more control over what they learn, and how and where they learn it and a period in which the institutional grip on accreditation has begun to loosen. Today's edupunks – a term used by Kamenetz

(2010) to describe the new, self-directed and self-determined learner – want to learn on their own terms. A transformation of higher education is unfolding – 'a colossal shift . . . toward informal and nontraditional learning pursuits chosen by the learner where much of the content is free and open' (Bonk, 2009, p. 40) – and new technologies are paving the way.

Heutagogy provides a theoretical framework for considering these systems in a holistic way, and the latest technologies serve as the agents for extending and supporting the framework. This chapter discusses emerging technologies that have triggered renewed interest in heutagogy and how these technologies support heutagogical practice.

Features of the new technologies

Web 2.0 is a common phrase used to describe the generation of internet technologies that arose after the first generation of the web. This second generation of web technology brought with it a wave of new user-friendly software that allows users to easily connect, collaborate, communicate, create content alone and in groups and to navigate the internet. Examples of Web 2.0 technology include blogs, wikis, social bookmarking and networking tools and other online collaboration tools. These technologies, emerging only in the last decade, have brought with them certain key features that support new forms of teaching and learning, allowing learners to become more active, more self-directed and more self-determined in their learning, as well as collaborating with others in the creation of new content. Table 4.1 shows primary key affordances of Web 2.0 features and includes some concepts developed by McLoughlin and Lee (2007).

These new synchronous and asynchronous technologies not only help learners become more self-directed in their learning, create new knowledge and become more digitally literate, but also help them to connect with learners from around the world to form communities of learning (Lee and McLoughlin, 2010, p 73). The learner decides with whom, how and where she or he will learn, with the technological features of this new system environment enabling 'practices such as collaborative content creation, peer assessment, formative evaluation of a learner's work, individual as well as group reflection on learning experiences, and up-to-date information regarding changes in collaborative spaces' (Duffy and Bruns, 2006, p. 1). These technologies also create a setting where heutagogy and self-directed learning can flourish.

Table 4.1 Web 2.0 features

Web 2.0 feature	How it works	Examples
Connectivity and social rapport (presence)/ communication	Supports creation of people networks and enables interaction among learners and instructors	Social networking (e.g. LinkedIn, Twitter, Facebook); MOOCs
Content discovery/ sharing (individually and collaboratively)	Gives learners the ability to search and discover information and share it with other learners	Social bookmarking (e.g. Del.icio.us, Diggo, StumbleUpon); social networking; Rich Site Summary (RSS) feeds; MOOCs
Content creation (individually and collaboratively)	Supports learners in actively creating new content as opposed to consuming content	Online collaboration (Google Docs); blogs, wikis, mashups
Knowledge and information aggregation and content modification	Supports learners in collection and customization of available information for personal use	Online collaboration (Google Docs), blogs, wikis, open educational resources (OERs), personal learning environments (PLEs)

Aligning new technology features with a heutagogical approach

[Heutagogy] suggests that learning is an extremely complex process that occurs within the learner, is unobserved and is not tied in some magical way to the curriculum. Learning is associated with making new linkages in the brain involving ideas, emotions, and experience that lead to new understanding about self or the world. Thus, learning occurs in random and chaotic ways and is a response to personal need and, often, occurs to resolve some ambiguity. (Hase, 2011, p. 2)

With this description in mind, heutagogy would seem to align particularly well with emerging Web 2.0 technologies. Heutagogy is fundamentally learner-centred, where the learner rather than the instructor determines the learning path. When using Web 2.0, the learner's ability to be self-determined is inherent in the system: the web is non-linear, allowing the learner to decide in a random way what and how she or he will learn. In addition to its non-linear structure, the web also offers opportunities for learners to create, connect, communicate and collaborate. Key attributes of heutagogy identified by Hase (2011) align well with Web 2.0 affordances and include double-loop learning, a focus on the

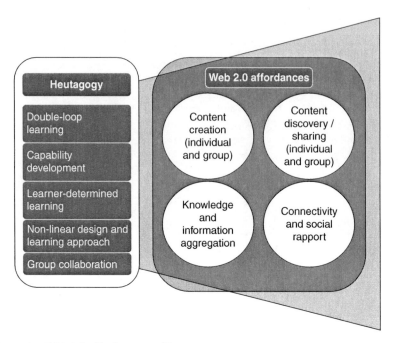

Figure 4.1 Web 2.0 affordances and heutagogy.

development of capability, a non-linear design and learning approach and group collaboration in the development of new knowledge (see Figure 4.1).

Self-determined learning

Self-determined learning is at the core of heutagogy. The web is conducive to and reinforces self-determined learning, as learners access the internet to find information, and hyperspace lets learners choose the path that they will take in learning. Online education makes learning available anytime and anywhere, and open educational resources (OERs), such as the MIT Open Courseware project (http://ocw.mit.edu/index.htm), the Khan Academy (www.khanacademy.org) and Harvard's Open Learning Initiative (www.extension.harvard.edu/open-learning-initiative), further extend learning opportunities and make course content readily and abundantly available to learners – and to teachers. In addition, different media platforms (YouTube, video, chat rooms, online forums) provide learners with the flexibility to choose where, how and what they will learn.

Within the Web 2.0 world, learning also becomes more informal and more social. Social, informal learning requires a shift from focusing on shaping the learning experience as a teacher, to modelling the experience as the learner's coach, and is more about connecting and collaborating with others than about controlling the learning process (Hart, 2012). Social networking tools such as blogs and Twitter have also been found to help students engage in the process of constructing a learning design together with their instructors and other students, resulting in a more learner-centred control of the learning process (Cameron and Tanti, 2011). Learners have become more empowered as learning has become more learner-centred, putting them in the position to take 'on the roles of teachers, and those formerly known as teachers are better positioned as guides, tutors, and mentors' (Bonk, 2009, p. 9).

Double-loop learning

Another important characteristic of heutagogy is double-loop learning, where learners confront their values and beliefs and adapt them accordingly, basing their decisions on the information available. In this process, learners 'try to find the most competent people for the decision to be made, and . . . try to build viable decision-making networks in which the major function of the group would be to maximize the contributions of each, so that when a synthesis was developed, the widest possible exploration of views would have taken place' (Argyris, 1976, p. 369).

Web 2.0 technologies support double-loop learning by providing an environment in which learners can connect with each other using a variety of platforms from social networking tools such as LinkedIn, academia.edu, Twitter and Facebook to social bookmarking tools such as Diigo, Evernote and Del. icio.u. Web 2.0 also supports the problem-solving process, as learners can use social media platforms to look for solutions (Google search). They can also ask for guidance (online forums, chat rooms and social networks), for example, by joining group discussions that allow them to explore a mix of different viewpoints, gathering information on the topic or topics that interest them, and reflecting upon and discussing problems and possible solutions within a group environment.

Double-loop learning also involves self-reflection on the individual learning process: reflection on what has been learned and how it has been learned. In this process of reflecting on how individual learning occurs, 'the learner connects the knowledge or skill to previous experience, integrates it fully in terms of value, and is able to actively use it in meaningful and even novel ways' (Hase,

2011, pp. 2–3). Within the Web 2.0 environment, blogs have long been found to be useful tools for supporting reflective practice, in addition to providing a platform to store resources that can be reflected upon later (Churchill, 2009; Mak et al., 2010; Yang, 2009).

Capability development

The next attribute of heutagogy is capability development. A learner exhibits capability when she or he is able to apply competencies in unique and different circumstances. Competency, according to Hase (2011), is about 'the past and is the ability to replicate a behaviour' (p. 3), whereas capability is the ability to transfer, adapt and even modify the competency when applying it in new environments. Hase illustrates the concept with an example of a worker who uses a hard hat at work – demonstrating competence in safety measures – but who does not exhibit the same competence at home while mowing the lawn in bare feet, without a hat or shirt in the glaring midday sun: the worker is thus competent, but not capable.

One cannot determine the moment when learning actually occurs and when a learner moves from competency to capability. Teachers can, however, provide opportunities for learners to exercise their competencies in order to develop capability, preparing learners to act on the learning moment when it arises. By teaching digital literacy skills, instructors can support the development of competencies so that learners can effectively navigate the web and use these skills to support self-determined learning and also to transfer these skills to new environments. Examples of Web 2.0 activities that can help students develop digital literacy skills include: having learners use Twitter to follow a scholar for a semester and then report the results by re-tweeting tweets and research of interest, using online mind maps both individually and in groups to create a web of ideas and concepts and having students create and contribute to individual blogs and to the blogs of their peers.

Non-linear design and learning approach

Heutagogy is further defined by its non-linear design and learning approach, an attribute that aligns seamlessly with the non-linear design of the web, which is characterized by a construct of hypertext topics and hyperlinks. This non-linear design transports learners to new information with just a click, allowing learners to define and determine their individual learning paths as they explore the web in search of new learning (Peters, 2010). Learning is no longer determined by time, place or person, and it is this freedom of choice that empowers the learner and that 'sets the Web of Learning apart from other forms of learning', helping learners 'make personal decisions related to their explorations and potential online discoveries . . . [and] develop a sense of ownership and . . . self-determination' (Bonk, 2009, p. 34).

Group collaboration

Heutagogy is also characterized by group collaboration, a common attribute of Web 2.0. While Web 1.0 promoted the passive consumption of information and the creation of knowledge, Web 2.0 is characterized by user design and the development of new information. There is an emphasis on active learning rather than passive learning, with learners creating their own content, and as a result becoming more engaged in the learning process (Blaschke et al., 2010). Tools are social and community-based, supporting the construction of individual and group knowledge (Duffy and Bruns, 2006). For example, Google Docs can be used for classroom projects, allowing learners to work together in building new content and knowledge over time. Wikis, such as Wikispaces and PBWorks, can be used in the same manner to create a community of learners that construct new knowledge in non-linear ways. LinkedIn groups and other social networks can support group collaboration and problem solving. In environments such as these, 'anyone can now learn anything from anyone at anytime' (Bonk, 2009, p. 6).

Negotiated assessment and models for delivery

In a heutagogical approach to teaching and learning, assessment and curricula need to be flexible and be negotiated between learner and teacher, and characterized by 'true collaboration regarding content and process between teacher and learner . . . [and] spontaneous and organic learning experiences' (Hase, 2011, p. 4). Because the learner, rather than the instructor, can be partially responsible for assessing learning, institutions of higher education have been somewhat hesitant in incorporating heutagogy into the classroom.

At the moment, however, higher education is experiencing the beginning of a transformation brought about by the new web technologies that are challenging established systems of teaching and learning. In this new open web, 'learning will be more customizable and specific to the learner's true needs, not prescribed by someone foreign to that student, classroom, school system, university, or culture' (Bonk, 2009, p. 47). Stanford professors are giving free lectures to learners who 'attend' their MOOCs; other universities taking up this approach include Princeton University, the University of Michigan and the University of Pennsylvania (Kolowich, 2012; Lewin, 2012a,b). Digital badges (obtained where a provider of learning gives digital badges to those who pass associated exams) are emerging as a means to assess learner skill and competency. Learners are driving the movement, becoming more actively involved in determining the learning process and conditions (Kamenetz, 2010; Stewart, 2012).

MOOCs are one delivery model that could create a bridge between education and practice, bringing together traditional forms of education with the non-traditional (Stewart, 2012). Anywhere from hundreds to thousands of learners can participate in a MOOC, where learners 'self-organize their participation according to learning goals, prior knowledge and skills, and common interests' and 'negotiate the extent and nature of their participation according to their individual needs and wishes' (McAuley et al., 2010, pp. 4–5). Using extensive open resources for teaching, an instructor facilitates the MOOC, while learners choose their learning path within the MOOC, becoming more independent as they create new social learning networks and a framework for lifelong learning (McAuley et al., 2010).

With digital, or open badges, learners can build individual educational plans, collecting badges to form a patchwork quilt of learning. Each badge represents the skills and competencies acquired by the learner and can help build communities of learners, support achievement of learning goals and document the learner path (O'Brien, 2011). Badges also have the potential to replace processes used for assessing prior learning, as well as to create opportunities for competency and skill training (Lewin, 2012b). The extent to which such approaches increase learner capability, an essential element of heutagogy, is yet to be determined.

The personal learning environment (PLE) or network (PLN) is another potential model for promoting self-determined learning. A PLE has been described as 'both a broad, holistic learning landscape and as a specific collection of tools that facilitate learning' (Martindale and Dowdy, 2010, p. 177). In a PLE, learners choose the tools that they incorporate into their learning network, incorporating information such as blogs, websites, wikis and social networking tools to construct a personalized learning environment. Wilson et al. (2007) envision the PLE as a model that supports lifelong learning and personalization, allows for symmetric connections and formal as well as informal learning, supports connections with people and information, lets learners take an active role in learning and promotes the filtering and channelling of information.

These new educational models, or systems of learning, provide an opportunity to not only support a self-determined approach to learning but also to bring change to education. In these models, learners learn how and what they want to learn and how they will be assessed, with some institutions now offering a form of certification but without the formal credit (Kolowich, 2012).

Guidelines for using Web 2.0 to support a heutagogical approach

Basic guidelines can be applied for incorporating Web 2.0 and social media to support a heutagogical approach in learning, based on the features offered by social media. These include:

1. Incorporating development of digital literacy skills in the classroom for the purposes of self-determined learning and active use of media for new content development. Development of certain competencies in digital literacy can contribute to the development of learner capability. Digital literacy skills include the ability to effectively search for, find and evaluate information, as well as to make connections across and contribute to the ongoing development of the digital system. Media should be used actively rather than passively with an emphasis on creation rather than consumption, that is, having learners create a video rather than just watch it, or have them create a wiki and contribute to the content rather than only read it. By promoting an approach where learners learn through discovery, teachers support 'the independent, self-determined and self-regulated acquisition of knowledge based on the learner's own strategies for searching, finding, selecting and applying' (Peters, 2010, p. 153).

2. Encouraging group collaboration and co-construction of knowledge. Communities of learning can be created within the classroom, as well as outside the classroom (e.g. using MOOCs). Learners can create their own communities using social networking tools or by using a wiki for constructing and aggregating knowledge.

3. Promoting reflection using online learning journals. Blaschke and Brindley (2011) found that learning journals can, 'provide real value in developing student skills for lifelong learning, while actively involving students in their individual learning processes by having them collect, organize, reflect on, and create content' (p. 7). Boud et al. (1985) recommended incorporating three elements for reflective practice: returning to experience, attending to feelings and re-evaluating the experience (p. 26). In addition, learners should be encouraged to not only reflect on what they have learned but also on the learning process they have undertaken and how this process has influenced their personal value system.

4. Scaffold the learning process as needed, especially for learners who are not yet fully autonomous. In their research on student-constructed learning design, Cameron and Tanti (2011) found that scaffolding learning activities helps guide the learning process and develop learners' metacognitive and communication skill, and is necessary in those cases where students lacked the essential skills of autonomous working. Incorporation of scaffolding in the form of guided questions, in particular, by asking learners to reflect on their thinking and learning processes, has also been found to further enhance reflective practice (Blaschke and Brindley, 2011).

5. Placing strong emphasis on formative and negotiated assessment. What is to be learned should be open to negotiation, and curriculum should be flexible. The learner should be actively involved in the learning process, with the instructor using Socratic practice to seek 'options and possibilities on which the participant can reflect and then make relevant choices' (Hase, 2011, p. 7). Ongoing formative assessment, with the instructor in the role of guide and counsellor, can also help support scaffolding of the learning process. If additional structure is needed, learning contracts built together with the learner can be used to structure the learning.

6. Encouraging exploration and experimentation. Once learners have mastered a competency, instructors can have them test out their newly acquired skill in new environments, for example, by having them apply the same competency or knowledge outside the classroom, such as in the learner's work environment. The web environment provides a multitude of opportunities for learners to search and explore ideas on their own.

7. Choosing an environment that supports learners in free and open learning. Learners should have the freedom to determine what they will learn and how they will learn it and the structure of the learning environment should encourage and promote this kind of learning. Learners should be able to

choose the kind of learning model – whether MOOC, digital badges or PLE – that best supports them in their pursuit of self-determined learning.

Conclusion

Bonk (2009) writes that 'technology by itself will not empower learners. Innovative pedagogy is required' (p. 33). Heutagogy has already been identified as an approach to learning within distance education, recognized by Anderson (2010) as a 'net-centric' theory that leverages certain technical features of the web, such as low-cost and powerful communication, information abundance and autonomous agents that help learners in the aggregation and synthesizing of information (Blaschke, 2012; Bonk, 2009, p. 33). The theory provides a methodological framework for describing and promoting the forms of learning occurring in the web environment and for navigating a new world reality of complexity, open and non-linear systems and unpredictable change (Hase, 2011). Web 2.0 technologies are inherently heutagogical in their design and approach to teaching and learning, and they create an environment that 'will probably be the most efficacious "enabler" of independent and self-determined learning' (Peters, 2010, p. 153). As higher education searches for meaningful ways of using new technologies, such as Web 2.0, in the classroom and for meeting the changing needs of its students, exploring the educational applications of heutagogy within the wider educational discipline has considerable merit.

References

Anderson, T. (2010), 'Theories for learning with emerging technologies', in G. Veletsianos (ed.), *Emerging Technologies in Distance Education*. Canada: Athabasca University Press, 23–40.

Argyris, C. (1976), 'Single-loop and double-loop models in research on decision making', *Administrative Science Quarterly*, 21, 363–75.

Blaschke, L. M. (2012), 'Heutagogy and lifelong learning: a review of heutagogical practice and self-determined learning', *International Review of Research in Open and Distance Learning*, 13(1), 56–71. Retrieved 29 November from: www.irrodl.org/index.php/irrodl/article/view/1076/2113.

Blaschke, L. M. and Brindley, J. (2011), 'Establishing a foundation for reflective practice: a case study of learning journal use', *European Journal of Open, Distance, and E-Learning (EURODL)*, Special Issue. Retrieved 29 November 2012 from: www.eurodl.org/materials/special/2011/Blaschke_Brindley.pdf.

Blaschke, L. M., Porto, S. and Kurtz, G. (2010), 'Assessing the added value of Web 2.0 tools for e-learning: the MDE experience', *Proceedings of the European Distance and E-Learning Network (EDEN) Research Workshop*, 25–27 October, Budapest, Hungary.

Bonk, C. J. (2009), *The World is Open: How Web Technology Is Revolutionizing Education*. San Francisco, CA: Jossey-Bass.

Boud, D., Keogh, R. and Walker, D. (1985), *Reflection: Turning Experience into Learning*. London: Kogan Page.

Cameron, L. and Tanti, M. (2011), 'Students as learning designers: using social media to scaffold the experience', *eLearning Papers*, 27. Retrieved 27 November 2012 from: http://elearningeuropa.info/sites/default/files/asset/papers_27_InD_3.pdf.

Churchill, D. (2009), 'Educational applications of web 2.0: using blogs to support teaching and learning', *British Journal of Educational Technology*, 40(1), 179–83.

Duffy, P. and Bruns, A. (2006), 'The use of blogs, wikis and RSS in education: a conversation of possibilities', *Proceedings Online Learning and Teaching Conference*, 31–8, Brisbane. Retrieved 27 November 2012 from: http://eprints.qut.edu.au.

Hart, J. (2012), '10 things to remember about social learning (and the use of social media for learning)' [Blog post]. *Learning in the Social Workplace*. Retrieved 27 November 2012 from: www.c4lpt.co.uk/blog/2012/03/23/10-things-to-remember-about-social-learning-and-the-use-of-social-media-for-learning/.

Hase, S. (2011), 'Learner defined curriculum: heutagogy and action learning in vocational training', *Southern Institute of Technology Journal of Applied Research*, Special Edition. Retrieved 27 November 2012 from: http://sitjar.sit.ac.nz/SITJAR/Special.

Hase, S. and Kenyon, C. (2000), 'From andragogy to heutagogy', *UltiBase*. Retrieved 27 November 2012 from: www.psy.gla.ac.uk/~steve/pr/Heutagogy.html.

Kamenetz, A. (2010), Edupunks, Edupreneurs, and the Coming Transformation of Higher Education. Canada: Chelsea Green Publishing Company.

Kolowich, S. (2012), 'Elite universities online play', *Insider Higher Ed*. Retrieved 27 November 2012 from: www.insidehighered.com/news/2012/04/18/princeton-penn-and-michigan-join-mooc-party.

Lee, M. J. W. and McLoughlin, C. (2010), 'Beyond distance and time constraints: applying social networking tools and Web 2.0 approaches to distance education', in G. Veletsianos (ed.), *Emerging Technologies in Distance Education*. Canada: Athabasca University Press. Retrieved 27 November 2012 from: www.aupress.ca/books/120177/ebook/04_Veletsianos_2010-Emerging_Technologies_in_Distance_Education.pdf.

Lewin, T. (2012a), 'Instruction for masses knocks down campus walls', *The New York Times*. Retrieved 27 November 2012 from: www.nytimes.com/2012/03/05/education/moocs-large-courses-open-to-all-topple-campus-walls.html?_r=1andpartner=rssandemc=rss.

—. (2012b), 'Beyond the college degree: online educational badges', *The New York Times*. Retrieved 27 November 2012 from: www.nytimes.com/2012/03/05/education/ beyond-the-college-degree-online-educational-badges.html?ref=education.

Mak, S., Williams, R. and Mackness, J. (2010), 'Blogs and forums as communication and learning tools in a MOOC', *Proceedings of the 7th International Conference on Networked Learning*, University of Lancaster, Lancaster. Retrieved 27 November 2012 from: www.lancs.ac.uk/fss/organisations/netlc/past/nlc2010/abstracts/PDFs/ Mak.pdf.

Martindale, T. and Dowdy, M. (2010), 'Personal learning environments', in G. Veletsianos (ed.), *Emerging Technologies in Distance Education*. Canada: Athabasca University Press. Retrieved 27 November 2012 from: www.aupress.ca/books/120177/ebook/09_ Veletsianos_2010-Emerging_Technologies_in_Distance_Education.pdf.

McAuley, A., Stewart, B., Siemens, G. and Cormier, D. (2010), 'Massive open online courses: digital ways of knowing and learning', *Knowledge Synthesis Grant on the Digital Economy*, sponsored by University of Prince Edward Island. Retrieved 27 November 2012 from: www.elearnspace.org/Articles/MOOC_Final.pdf.

McLoughlin, C. and Lee, M. J. W. (2007), 'Social software and participatory learning: pedagogical choices with technology affordances in the Web 2.0 era', *Proceedings of Ascilite Conference*, 2–5 December, Singapore. Retrieved 27 November 2012 from: www.ascilite.org.au/conferences/singapore07/procs/mcloughlin.pdf.

O'Brien, A. (2011), 'Student awards: digital badges make a debut' [Blog post]. *Edutopia*. Retrieved 27 November 2012 from: www.edutopia.org/blog/digital-badges-student- awards-anne-obrien.

Peters, O. (2010), Distance Education in Transition: Developments and Issues. Oldenburg, Germany: BIS-Verlag.

Stewart, B. (2012). 'Forget the business case: open online courses are about learning', *The Guardian*. Retrieved 27 November 2012 from: www.guardian.co.uk/higher- education-network/blog/2012/apr/16/forget-business-online-courses-learning.

Wilson, S., Liber, O., Johnson, M., Beauvoir, P., Sharples, P. and Milligan, C. (2007), 'Personal learning environments: challenging the dominant design of education systems', *Journal of E-Learning and Knowledge Society*, 3(2). Retrieved 27 November 2012 from: http://services.economia.unitn.it/ojs/index.php/Je-LKS_EN/article/ view/247.

Yang, S. H. (2009),'Using blogs to enhance critical reflection and community of practice', *Educational Technology and Society*, 12(2), 11–21. Retrieved 27 November 2012 from: www.ifets.info/journals/12_2/2.pdf.

5

Applying the Principles of Heutagogy to a Postgraduate Distance-Learning Programme

Trevor Kerry

Summary

The aim of this chapter is to explore the concept of heutagogy and to investigate the ways in which adult learners (specifically teachers and education managers) who were taking a masters level course by distance learning, could take control of their own learning.

Introduction

My interest in heutagogy could be said to have been an evolution of thought and practice rather than a revolution brought about by sudden insight. Having been involved in distance tutoring of the MSc course at Leicester University, United Kingdom, for some 16 years, I had evolved ways of working to make tutoring more effective. These were, in part, ways of thinking about teaching at a distance, and in part changes imposed externally, for example by technology, where the postal system has been replaced by email. What continued to exercise my professional interest was a question: how can I go on improving my service to students so that they learn more effectively in a distance context? It should be said unequivocally that my interest was in students' learning (both now and into the future) rather than in students' learning of the course (immediate materials) – though the level at which they achieve the latter is, of course, important both to them and to me.

Like many distance courses, ours depends on students accessing materials and completing assignments. For a distance tutor the challenge was how to go beyond simply commenting on drafts of work so as to build learning skills into the study process. My approach had been to develop a technique for analysing assignment drafts, which guided students through challenging questions rather than through didactic commentary. With the introduction of email, a collection of potential attachments was developed on the lines of FAQs (frequently asked questions) on websites. Using these speeded up the process of teaching students simple techniques, and meant that commentary on the draft work submitted by students could concentrate on making learning demands and challenging their thinking. Commentary was often in the form of questions rather than guidance. But what was also important were other factors about the approach to the tutorial interchange. These factors were:

Speed: Students appreciate a speedy response: if they are working today they don't want a response in a week's time.

Tone: Language has to signal a rapport with the individual and to avoid any suggestion of condescension by an 'expert' to a 'novice'.

Use of student expertise: Students are professionals with a high level of responsibility, and therefore it is critical to recognize and use their extant knowledge and expertise

Learning alongside: Flows from the previous item; it is critical that a tutor signals an ability and open-ness to also learning new skills and information

Encouraging independence: Much commentary may need to be couched more in questions than in answers: real learning is about challenge

Pastoral concern: The distance tutor must be just as much of a friend, counsellor and adviser as a face-to-face tutor would be.

Together, these approaches began to look like a 'system' for conducting distance learning; and it was at the stage of thinking that an encounter with the work of Kenyon and Hase (2010) began to formulate these ideas into a heutagogical approach.

The research

While informal feedback suggested that the course fitted with this theory, there was no empirical evidence to support the making of such a claim. By seeking the views of our students it was hoped to test the overall claim and also to refine views of the extent to which the principles of heutagogy were being achieved in the course. The intention was to apply the outcomes to our work with students, and (potentially) more widely across the whole MSc Ed Leadership offering from the university.

The following research questions were developed to these ends:

- To what extent do students recognize the main principles of heutagogy to be present in their learning experience?
- How are these principles exemplified in the five main areas of the course?
- What more might be done to promote a heutagogical approach within this degree course?
- Within their current employment, what benefits have students gained through these principles and the course in their professional learning?

Background

The MSc course comprises three 'taught' modules each of which consists of a set of course materials on a theme resulting in an investigative assignment written with tutorial support. Students then choose a title, which is pursued through a Research Methods module; and that in turn is expanded into a 20,000-word dissertation. Students have a choice of themes, which consist of topics such as leadership, human resource management, managing finance and policy in education – the exact range of available modules alters slightly over time but all have a leadership/management focus. Students may also choose to write a literature-based assignment in place of one investigation. The titles of all assignments are open to student choice with tutorial advice, though the choice in each case has to align with the theme being studied.

At the time of undertaking this research my tutorial group consisted of 27 students at various stages of the course. In addition I had records of 16 students who had successfully completed the course. In the degree course the final dissertation is graded (pass grades are A, B, C). Of the students in the cohort who had reached the end of the course (known as 'Completers'), 50 per cent had completed at grade A, 31.25 per cent at grade B and 18.75 per cent at grade C. Of these 16, 13 of the most recent completers were selected to be the population for the completion cohort; and the remaining three were identified as the group with whom to pilot the instrument. In addition to the completers, 27 current students were available to participate, labelled 'Continuers', and 23 of them did participate.

Investigation and methodology

A survey instrument was developed in the form of an emailed questionnaire, which was designed to gather data about the extent to which heutagogical principles could be, and were, adhered to during the course. This method of data collection was deemed appropriate because it mirrored the means of working that the students had been used to during the actual course. So that students had a reference source on heutagogy to assist in answering questions on the course, they were provided with a sheet of initial background information, illustrated in Box 5.1.

Box 5.1 Initial background information about heutagogy

Please read this before you begin

Pedagogy, andragogy and heutagogy are essentially theories of educating.

Pedagogy sees the learner as dependent on the educator who decides what, where and when the student will learn. It is common in schools.

Andragogy refers to adult learning that is partially self-directed. It calls for an emphasis on educational process rather than content, where the curriculum needs to be given relevance, modes of teaching promote discovery and the different backgrounds of students are recognized in designing teaching and curriculum.

Heutagogy is an extension of, rather than a replacement for, pedagogy and andragogy. Heutagogy displays certain principles about learning/educating which are absent from pedagogy, and often from andragogy. These include the following eight characteristics or dimensions:

1. Learning when the learner is ready: the learner largely controls the process of learning, making their own decisions about pace and activity according to need and interest.
2. Learning is seen as a complex process requiring the learner to move beyond knowledge and skills – it is not regurgitation, copying, modelling (though these things may happen). It requires new connections and more inventive insights to be made.
3. Learning does not depend on the teacher and can be triggered by an experience beyond the control of the teacher, that is, it becomes self-directed.
4. Learning is focused on the student not on a syllabus: it is about what the student wants to know and chooses to explore.

Learning results in an expanding capability to learn for one's self: to direct and control one's own learning and its directions, which in turn leads to:

5. *Self-sufficiency in learning:* the confidence to explore avenues, take risks and know how to find things out.
6. *Reflexivity:* the ability to take on board the implications of learning, absorb these into one's own situation, to change ways of thinking and ways of acting as a result of learning.
7. *Applicability of what is learned:* so that connections are made with professional and other lives beyond 'theory alone'.
8. *Positive learning values:* so that learning becomes a pleasurable experience to be indulged in for its own sake.

Heutagogy certainly requires more commitment from the educator/teacher than does a conventional approach to learning. *Teachers take on more of the role of facilitator* or mentor using this approach so that they can continually be evaluating what the needs of the student might be. Teachers should feel challenged by the prospect of working *with* students (rather than having the students working *for* staff).

The instrument asked respondents about eight key factors of heutagogy and did so for each of the five core elements of the course (course materials, distance tutoring, assignment writing, writing the research methods assignment and production of the final dissertation). A small amount of additional demographic data was collected, and there were four opportunities for the respondents to comment about the course, about the heutagogical principles themselves, and on how either of these had affected their work and careers (Box 5.2).

Before proceeding with the research, permission was obtained from the MSc Programme Director to approach students; the anonymity of participants was guaranteed. The instrument was piloted using three students who had completed the course and had graduated the longest time ago. As a result of the pilot phase, a minor change was made to the instructions for the questionnaire, clarifying that answers longer than one sentence were fully acceptable.

The final sample was divided into completers and continuers, a total of 43 students. Four students were omitted, either because they were too new to have formed accurate impressions of the course, or were having problems with their studies (e.g. due to health issues).

Box 5.2 A sample of part of the survey instrument

This box is about the **STUDY MATERIALS**

Please fill in the right-hand box for EACH item (S1–S8) listed. In each case, read the left-hand box and then please do two things:

1. Answer Yes/No as appropriate (you can delete the one which does NOT apply) – then please

2. Supply a reason and/or example to illustrate your answer

S1 The study materials allow/encourage you to learn when you, as learner, are ready	Yes	No
S2 The study materials ask you to use complex processing skills to achieve learning	Yes	No
S3 When using the study materials the focus of learning is on you, the learner, not on the syllabus	Yes	No
S4 The study materials trigger learning experiences beyond the control of the teacher	Yes	No
S5 Using the study materials, your learning results in: • Increased self-sufficiency in your learning	Yes	No
S6 Using the study materials, your learning results in: • Reflexivity on your part	Yes	No
S7 Using the study materials, your learning results in: • Greater applicability in what is learned to your personal situation	Yes	No
S8 Using the study materials, your learning results in: • Your feeling positively about your learning (even when it is difficult)	Yes	No

---

Analysis

In analysing the data from the students it seemed to make most sense first to set down the data from the completers, and then to compare and contrast the data with that from the continuers.

The completers

All the completers were asked to answer five sections each consisting of eight questions, with each question requesting a Yes/No answer followed by some narrative comment.

Study materials

In 87.5 per cent of cases respondents thought that the study materials related to the MSc course supported heutagogical principles. Respondents said the study materials, '[provided] growth and empowerment'.

They went on to say the following: 'You make connections in your head to apply to a particular situation and connect different arguments together to form your own ideas'; 'You feel good when it makes sense and you move to a new level of understanding'; 'A high level of maturity and independence was assumed [by the materials]'; 'Different styles of writing in the study materials, along with different tasks to be completed . . . ensure that a variety of processing skills are called upon'; 'A high degree of autonomy is given to the student, and the vast resources of the internet mean that students are able to find new resources to support their research'; 'Every learner processes the information . . . differently and, as a result, has personal learning experiences which are beyond the control of the tutor'; '[They made] the student reflect on his particular situation at all times'; '[They] give you just the key to open more doors to learning'; 'You can study at your own pace selecting the direction you wish your studies to take . . . however, this entails increased responsibility on the student's part and a certain maturity'; and 'The materials are really just prompts for you to reflect and build on'.

There were a couple of dissenting voices; one said, 'I'm not sure I've changed my ways of thinking or acting!' Another asserted that, 'Whilst the materials allowed me to be very reflective about my own teaching practices, I never really spent much time reflecting on my main learning, especially in terms of skills and knowledge.'

Tutorial input

Some students had had experience of working with up to three tutors. The scores suggested that this aspect of the MSc programme is considered as powerfully in tune with heutagogical principles. Narrative comments indicate that tutorial activities 'Helped me grow in confidence and vocabulary'; 'Are self-driven and fulfilled with eagerness'; and 'Meant guidance was given but the action had to come from me!'

Tutor guidance was considered to be important because,

I tackled issues that were very relevant to me; and my tutor always helped me to better understand and express my ideas. I was trained to think deeper into facts and not simply to mention issues which I came across in the literature. I began to see my studies make more sense.

Another said 'I found the feedback . . . very motivating and re-assuring' and

> I learned how to gather and present information in different ways which I had not done before. My tutor was there for me and continuously supported and guided me. I was able [through tutoring] to link the different parts of my research in ways I did not think possible previously.

> Tutor feedback always prompted further study and reflection which sometimes took my studies in unexpected and interesting directions.

> I learned a lot of new research skills just by being nudged in the right direction. Questions posed by my tutor encouraged me to apply skills to my personal situation and made work much more relevant. I have sometimes felt frustrated when I think I've finished something and then my tutor poses another question! But this eventually improves my work and gives me much more satisfaction.

Only one student felt he hadn't 'changed his ways of thinking and acting' and averred that, 'I felt that the focus was still on the syllabus'.

The writing process

Writing assignments were deemed overwhelmingly (90.4%) to be in tune with heutagogical principles. One student declared that, 'Writing epitomised heutagogy, there is a total focus on the learner. There is an exciting independence and sense of accomplishment that emerges during the writing.'
Other comments were:

> Although deadlines are set, these are sufficiently long-range to allow mature learners . . . flexibility and freedom.

> Lots of complicated elements of reasoning and argument are required in the writing.

> My tutor's feedback notes, the course structure and literature always gave me the opportunity to develop an issue or topic which was very relevant to my working/ learning experience which altogether made me feel I was the focus.

And, of course, because students chose, subject to approval, their own topics:

> Written assignments could be focused on a particular interest; it allowed the skills of writing, rather than the content, to be the learning focus.

Another student focused on the progression that writing allowed:

> Every assignment I completed I felt that I was moving to new knowledge areas, which was a very fulfilling experience.

Despite the time limits for assignments, a student commented that there was still time to reflect, another said the actual writing had to be developmental, concise and objective, and another student had voluntarily spent time attending relevant seminars – and none of this was prescribed by the course.

Research Methods Assignment (RMA)

The RMA is best described as preparation for composing the first three chapters of the final dissertation – the Statement of the Research Problem, the Review of Literature and the Methodology. While other elements of the programme hover at around 90 per cent positive scores, the RMA managed a strong, but lower, 73 per cent. One student who considered that the subject did not meet the heutagogical approach said:

> I think that the focus is more on the various approaches and research tools because you need to understand and know how and when to apply them before you embark on the dissertation itself.

However, the majority made comments along these lines:

> It was very challenging yet very exciting to use all my processing skills to gather, analyse and integrate data from so many sources and authors . . . It definitely increased self-sufficiency in my learning as I had to continuously look for new data and manage that information in a way that would benefit my research . . . I felt very positive and excited, as my research was taking me to another dimension of thinking and applying my knowledge in my personal and professional life.

Perhaps if the RMA does not fully meet the criteria of heutagogy, it is due to a failure of explanation and of understanding rather than of process. This explanation is reinforced when one looks at student comments on the whole of the dissertation writing process (which subsumes the RMA skills), and which was rated the strongest element of the course in terms of heutagogical principles.

Dissertation

Of the 104 scores for dissertations matching with heutagogical principles, 96.2 per cent were positive. The following sums up the situation for all the students:

> At the heart of any dissertation lies the discussion that ensues from the project's findings as it is counterpoised with the arguments presented in the literature review. Reflectivity is what gives life to the whole discussion. Even more so

than with writing and RMA, the objectives and level of research achieved in a dissertation will only be truly relevant if applied in practice. Better still it should be shedding light on a relevant area of study which results in a tangible practical local 'improvement' . . . Love for learning is probably one of the reasons for furthering study in the first place. The learning process itself generates positive feelings, albeit peppered with the not uncommon spates of frustration as one comes to grips with the required skills. This eventually culminates with the application of learning into practice, particularly when this results in improvement initiatives.

Summary

These respondents represent those who had successfully completed the MSc programme. While it may be argued that their experience cannot be generalized, the core messages are clear. The MSc Distance Learning programme in educational leadership does lend itself to heutagogical principles and fulfils them in practice. The exceptions centre around the RMA, and the problem there may not lie in the nature of the task but rather in the way it is presented.

The continuers

Anyone who had not completed the course (i.e. who had undertaken only the assignment writing module) was asked to answer three sections, each consisting of eight questions, with each question requesting a Yes/No answer followed by some commentary. No statistical claims are made for the quantitative data except that they demonstrate, in a very immediate way, the basic trends in the answers. The data are substantially positive, indicating a course that meets heutagogical criteria.

Study materials

In 87 per cent of cases the continuer group thought that the study materials related to the MSc programme supported heutagogical principles. Respondents said the study materials, 'Spark curiosity that leads you to experiment and thus experience new things that are not under the tutor's control'. One said that:

> You find yourself reasoning and critically reflecting upon theories and concepts as understood by others and ending up deliberating on where you stand compared to them . . . the study material provided me with an identity of my own, in the sense that I could decide on what to focus upon.

One person said the study materials produced 'an on-going process of reflexivity', while for another it was more a question of personal engagement by transitioning to a self-sufficient mode of learning.

Despite a few reservations, the materials were viewed as heutagogically sound, and as fulfilling their role effectively.

Tutorial input

While 89 per cent commented positively, a handful responded 'yes' and 'no' indicating that that they found the heutagogical approach in some aspects but not in others. One student found the tutorial process both liberating and demanding, commenting that,

> I feel I have time to think, investigate further and work at a pace I can manage . . . as my tutor responds quickly but does not impose time constraints on me beyond the deadlines given for each assignment [students have six months for each module]. My tutor encourages me to analyse, synthesis and summarise! Ouch!

One student considered that 'the nature of the programme allows me continually to change the way I think, analyse and learn'. Another said: 'my tutor did not just talk about the course but also about what I was going through and what I wanted to achieve'. Another stated: 'guidance from my tutor is on-going, which makes me positive. Shortcomings are ironed out throughout the work, not at the last minute'. Another believed that queries were handled sympathetically by the tutor and that the tutor encouraged him/her 'to have ownership of my own knowledge'. All of these comments – and many more like them – support the heutagogical soundness of tutoring in this course.

Almost half of the negative comments for this element of the course came from one individual. Clearly, he/she had a negative opinion on tutorial work, to the extent of claiming not to understand what tutoring was.

Students who sign up for the MSc are in no doubt that this is a 'distance' course. They stay in touch with their tutor by email. The frequency of email traffic is controlled by the student, they can make contact as often as they wish. Drafts of work are read and commented on assiduously; individual queries requiring one sentence answers can be directed to the tutor at any time. Tutors may enquire after a student who has gone 'off the radar' for a long period, but person-to-person contact beyond email is not a part of the degree contract.

The writing process

The results for assignment writing mirror those for study materials and tutorial input and indicate strong positive outcomes.

One student described themselves as having linear thought processes and to have found the assignment writing 'very engaging'. He/she suggested that free choice of topic within the module theme, and the fact that the tutor encouraged this, meant that the process was highly heutagogical, full of 'learning opportunities provoked only by the learners themselves'.

Another said that in his/her head he/she was 'always asking questions now' as a result of thinking through assignment approaches. There was positive comment about writing the literature review sections of the work, about having to search through models, having to analyse relationships and make sense of patterns and about having to apply the writing to one's own situation in the workplace. Many spoke of initial reticence, but of eventual confidence and self-sufficiency. One person pointed to the open-ended nature of investigative assignments – the fact that you did not know at the beginning where the work would lead. Another thought that each time an assignment was completed the student was able to 'push him/herself a little more'. Yet another suggested that assignments 'create a strong sense of purpose' even though writing was a lonely process, and he/she would have preferred to work in a group.

Continuers and completers compared

Both completer and continuer groups were extremely positive and consistent in their assessment that the MSc followed the principles of heutagogy. The slightly higher scores of completers may be because they could look back on a job finished, while the continuers were still finding their way around some of the learning processes. The strength of feeling, and the consistent and recurrent nature of the comments about the value of the course as a heutagogical experience, are very notable.

Discussion

The first research question asked: To what extent do students recognize the main principles of heutagogy to be present in their learning experience in the course? All the data – indicative scores and the overwhelming quantity of positive comments – indicate that the students did indeed recognize heutagogical principles as being a central feature of this course.

The second research question dealt with examples of whether and how students were pursuing heutatgogical learning principles in their work: How are these principles exemplified in the five main areas of the course, that is, course materials, distance tuition, assignment writing, the RMA unit and the dissertation?

We have seen that all of the five areas of the MSc were considered by the students to be substantially in line with heutagogical principles. Their comments have supported Kenyon and Hase's (2010) notion of adult learning, that it should be 'emergent, adaptive and natural'. Student comments have shown that most were openly 'engaged with their topic and emotionally excited by it' (p. 170). Learners were constructing 'their own meanings of the world based on their engagements with it' (Kenyon and Hase, 2010, p. 170). There were hints that the course gave students space to 'juggle the balls of their complex lives, while helping to develop the dispositions, knowledge and skills required of learners and employees in the twenty-first century', as suggested by Ashton and Elliott (2007).

However, while scores and comments indicate a positive approach across the board, the area of least enthusiasm for the students was that of the RMA. The grounds of these less positive feelings seem to be fourfold. The RMA emphasizes two skills above all others: reviewing literature and compiling a methodology – it is thus more theoretical and less practical than, say, assignment writing where actual research happens and there are tangible findings. The format of the RMA is constrained by the University – it may be no more constrained than other elements of the course but it is differently constrained, but that creates the impression of control. As the University takes tighter apparent control, the student has less control. In the opinion of some students, the purpose and rationale of the RMA is inadequately explained.

These observations lead us to research question three: What more might be done to promote a heutagogical approach within this degree course? The most obvious answer is to bring the RMA in line with the other elements of the course. As there are many positive opinions expressed about the RMA, the way forward is to take a cue from these. Simply put: those students for whom 'the penny drops' and they perceive the purpose of the RMA, find it valuable. For the rest, what is lacking is a really effective rationale. The University needs to consider re-appraising the Handbook guidance to articulate more effectively how this element of the course can be true to heutagogical principles.

The final research question probed whether students saw the course as advancing them professionally. The question asked: What benefits have students gained through these principles and the course in their professional learning within their current employment situation? Most of the continuer group either filed a nil response or said it was too early to say. Of those who responded with specific statement, the advantages gained were listed as:

- Becoming more reflective and more ambitious
- Providing different perspectives
- Improving contributions to meetings
- Implanting a real desire for a management post
- Encouraging the individual to make applications for promoted posts.

The completer group was, understandably, more specific. Some said they had had no change of role, but almost half were actively seeking, or had gained, a promotion. They reported:

- Increased confidence in their current roles
- Increased sympathy with the Senior Management Team's (SMT) problems
- Improved performance in their current roles
- Promotion to teaching and learning adviser post
- Encouragement to apply for an SMT post
- Promotion to assistant or deputy headship.

Conclusion

Stephenson (www.johnstepenson.net/staffs.ppt/) suggests that learning works well in e-contexts when three conditions are fulfilled: learners have the ability to learn for themselves; learners have belief in their personal power to learn; and they exercise powers of judgement. This small-scale research suggests that these conditions prevail in the Leicester MSc in Educational Leadership by distance learning. The research also suggests that, as far as students were concerned, there was an overwhelmingly positive view, which recognized the heutagogical principles embedded in the course, and students had a clear recognition of how they could benefit from those principles. Probably the most satisfying outcome is that students are now applying the principles of heutagogical learning to their own teaching and their own educational contexts. Changing minds is, in the end, more important than changing courses.

Internet reference

www.johnstepenson.net/staffs.ppt/.

References

Ashton, J. and Elliott, R. (2007), 'Juggling the balls – study, work, family and play: student perspectives on flexible and blended heutagogy', *European Early Childhood Education Research Journal*, 15(2), 167–81.

Kenyon, C. and Hase, S. (2010), 'Andragogy and heutagogy in postgraduate work', in T. Kerry, *Meeting the Challenges of Change in Postgraduate Education.* London: Continuum, 165–77.

6

Workplace Learning for Nurses

Mike Ramsay, John Hurley and Gavin R. Neilson

Summary

This chapter concerns the application of heutagogy to undergraduate pre-registration nurse education. Therein, there are a number of areas to consider and, indeed, challenges to surmount prior to witnessing the educational emergence of heutagogy as a preferred ethos and approach in the field. The clinical practice element, inherent within undergraduate pre-registration nursing courses, appears as an ideal arena to focus ideas about broadening the self-learning capabilities of the students. This can open up a vista of personal learning, knowledge application and personal development, alongside the traditional need for skills acquisition, gaining experience and professional socialization. Further, we propose that this approach can help those assessing the competency of students to practice acquired skills and apply related knowledge, as they can additionally appraise the student's ability to both see and negotiate their own learning needs and goals.

Heutagogy in professional education

Nursing is not dissimilar to other emergent professions, such as occupational therapy and social work, where vocational degrees are destination qualifications, combined with a licence to practice. These professions all seek to engage the successful graduate onto a path of life-long learning and, therefore, employing an ethos of heutagogy in undergraduates can arguably ease the transitions into professionally qualified practice and further job-related skills and knowledge acquisition (NMC, 2002; SEHD, 2006). In other words, applying heutagogical principles in undergraduates is a transferrable skills-set that may be a hallmark of graduateness and instil the confidence in new practitioners to self-select their future developmental learning experiences. Walker (1995 as cited in Glover et al., 2002) in identifying the features of graduateness saw four domains of task management and problem-solving; cooperative working, communication and self-awareness. These domains also fit well with the ability to self-identify, negotiate and enable learning inherent within heutagogy and can be seen as fitting well with skills and experiential learning requirements of curricula (Glover et al., 2002). Such alignment between student learning needs and their course requirements, plus bridging the learner to qualified practitioner transition, can mean that employing heutagogy with undergraduate nursing students equips them well for not only successful navigation of their studies but also for their future careers.

Barriers and challenges to enacting heutagogical learning in nursing education

Within nursing contexts the concept of heutagogy is embryonic, with very little theoretical discussion and even less formal application of its principles within the profession. Scope for the greater integration of heutagogy within nursing certainly exists, particularly given its powerful influence of learning from professional practice (Hase and Kenyon, 2000). However, careful consideration of the characteristics of nursing practice in general, and in workplace learning settings in particular, must be undertaken to successfully situate heutagogy into a diverse and, at times, seemingly contradictory nursing profession.

Many students need guidance to be successful heutagogical learners and must somehow be found a place within an arguably already overcrowded undergraduate curriculum. Canning (2010) offers some insights into the underpinning steps within this preparation. By creating a progressive student-based capability hierarchy moving onwards from being pedagogy-capable to heutagogy-capable, it is made apparent that educators must build learners' capabilities to enable them to be leaders of their own learning. While seemingly nuanced, this focus on developing the learner rather than their nursing capabilities would represent a landmark shift of emphasis by nurse education. While much is made of learner attributes within undergraduate curricula, an arguable truth is that nurse education remains highly regulated and controlled, primarily focused on clinical competency achievement, as distinct from personal capability development.

Use of simulators is perhaps the fastest growing field of healthcare education and is also a clear example of the character of nursing's preferred educative process. Simulation as a key underpinning of nurse education clearly demonstrates the preference for a fixed, predictable and tutor-led learning agenda that focuses upon behavioural/psychomotor objective attainment. Increasingly sophisticated technology enables nurse educators to set up clinical situations that reflect the realities of practice and hence permit clinical skill development within safe and controlled environments (NMC, 2007a). These can build student confidence and a foundation of clinical skill that subsequent practice-based learning could rapidly build upon. The use of simulators, however, is also mechanizing what once was a prized interpersonal-focused understanding of what nursing is and of the nurse education process itself. Berragan (2011) in her balanced critique on use of simulation certainly offers a voice of concern that preparing nurses needs less emphasis by nurse educators on the operational and technological aspects of the use of simulators, with more focus on affective capabilities and nurse identity formation.

While heutagogy and clinical simulators are not necessarily educationally mutually exclusive, there is a confluence of factors that certainly challenge the implementation of heutagogy within nursing curricula. Not least of these is that undergraduate nurses require leadership capabilities to self-direct their learning.

Leadership in practice-based learning

The historical and cultural nature of the nursing profession is one that underprepares nurses to be leaders, particularly early career, and even then only in response to the needs of the organization (Paterson et al., 2010). Nursing is a profession evolved from military and religious origins, each steeped in hierarchy and following the orders and instructions of more senior staff (Stanley and Sherratt, 2010). This lack of traditionally instilling leadership capability within nursing students creates a capability gap to the autonomy and reflexivity that is inherent within heutagogy. Indeed, nursing curricula generally reflects conformity and predictability with education and training formats set out as descriptive plans that intend nursing students to learn the preset product of core competencies combined with the process of critical reflection. Without specific tutor direction there appears little opportunity for new undergraduate nurses to challenge this from the classroom or lecture theatre given the established layers of power, tradition and legislative requirements that influence curricula in such settings. Therefore, clinical placements seemingly offer the greatest potential to utilize the adult-focused learning potential of heutagogy, as well as being the more likely environment from which to enact it.

Over the last 30 years nursing as a profession and, therefore, its higher education providers, has often framed what needs to be known by practicing nurses around the now seminal four ways of knowing (Carper, 1978). This schema identifies the knowledge domains of the empirical, personal, ethical and aesthetic. It could be argued that, in a reductionist fashion, nursing (in common with other healthcare professions) has latched firmly onto the empirical way of knowing. Such is the seemingly ongoing drive for evidence-based (often research-based in reality) practice: a hunger for the application of nursing interventions founded upon knowledge derived from science (Northington et al., 2005). Arguably this means the other three ways, and potentially more personal are neglected, thence care can become a series of mechanistic and compassionless science-born tasks.

Nurses mentoring students will therefore impart knowledge that is scientifically born, meeting the dominant driver. The other three ways of knowing may be only chanced upon by students in the classroom and in practice environments. Adoption of heutagogy can offset this skewed emphasis allowing students to balance out the undoubted need for application of scientific knowledge and its influence in treatment, with the more personal and perhaps person-centred facets of learning. This can result in the development of learning in-the-round by offering educational encounters, or the traditional nursing ideal of holistic learning (Northington et al., 2002) which enhances learner ability to deliver good care.

Central to embedding heutagogy is for mentors and nurse educators to possess the skills, values and attitudes that allow the fostering and support of self-generated learning in the clinical environment, which is so pivotal to heutagogy. Without this, students will be guided in traditional ways and will doubtlessly continue to meet the set criteria or competency tick-lists in their attainment record (Tiwari et al., 2005) but without necessarily exploring the width and depth of learning experience and perhaps not understand it fully. In short, both mentors and nurse educators have to lead the students to be leaders of their own learning (Hurley et al., 2012). Such leadership is not students directing others or assuming responsibility beyond capability but is about having a passion for nursing, enacting integrity and displaying self-confident behaviours (Carroll, 2006). Leadership within challenging health working environments is being able to identify and seize upon the unpredictable, link the unpredicted opportunity to self-identified required learning and then to navigate through the contexts and people within that learning situation. This seemingly requires assertiveness, advanced communication and self-awareness, as well as empathy and reflexivity (Hurley et al., 2012). Heutagogy in nursing clinical environments calls upon the nurse to have a clear idea of their self-leadership and to act in a manner that is congruent with the values of the profession (Barron and Hurley, 2012).

Can heutagogy improve nurse education?

A fundamental question in attempting to overcome the barriers challenging heutagogy within nursing contexts is – is it worth the effort? Without there being clear potential benefit for improving clinical outcomes and nursing practice generally there is likely to be limited appetite to address the issues discussed previously. Given that practice-based learning setting appears to offer best potential we shall focus upon that learning arena to highlight the worth of integrating heutagogy.

To competently practice in healthcare means ability in its professional graduates is needed to adjust ably to rapidly developing environments, knowledge and technological applications. Nursing, of course, is not immune from such developmental educational imperatives and as such future health services will need nurses with sophisticated skills. Some key drivers exist in Westernized economies (in particular). First, a growing and altered demographic population including many more elderly people is emerging; with all the complex healthcare requirements inherent with advancing years. Secondly, there are increased healthcare demands such as the expanding HIV epidemic and the impact of new or re-emergent diseases and infections. Thirdly, increased problems of addiction, violence and abuse will require extensive nursing input. Further, changes in public with greater consumer expectations of healthcare systems (bringing increasingly articulate and informed patients demanding more of care professionals) and lack of access to services among the indigent and homeless will also create even greater demands for nurses. All of these factors contribute to an increasingly complex set of learning capabilities – knowledge, practice, skills and attitudes (Cowan et al., 2005) – for students and equally a skilled response from their practice mentors and link lecturers in universities.

An opportunity and challenge exists for practice-based learning in nursing between the lecturer and mentor roles. Brown et al. (2005) emphasize that students place high value upon lecturer placement visits, despite being unable to identify their expectations around these. This can mean a situation ripe for exploitation of linking theoretical knowledge to practical contexts, with heutagogy as the potential facilitating factor in how students make more meaningful sense of these two key strands (theory and practice) that influence their learning. Equally, and somewhat paradoxically, however, Owen et al. (2005) highlight additional issues of lecturers being in clinical settings: with loss of lecturer clinical competencies and clinical staff's perceptions of them now lacking clinical credibility, the role of link lecturer can be seen as unwanted and undermined. Also apparent is that attempts to re-engage lecturers in clinical roles, and consequently regaining clinical credibility, are fraught with either organizational or individual lecturer-based challenges, plus tensions generated when lecturers challenge less than optimal practice. These challenges can possibly be ameliorated or removed altogether if the link lecturer can carve an educative niche to nurture theoretical knowledge and its interface with practice, rather than solely visiting to role-model, question or consider practice and competency attainment opportunities.

Again one can see the potential of heutagogy as an appropriate learning vehicle, dually encouraged by link lecturers and mentors, geared to accessing and applying the universal theory within a field, allowing student-led exploration of its fit with the practice context, the student's existing skills-base and the identification and comprehension of applying theory to skills yet to be acquired, thereby providing a clear path for ongoing student-centred reflection and learning. This allows link lecturers to encourage critical reflection on putting theory into practice, such as understanding theory practice gaps, identifying learning solely born out of practice or what Franks (2004) terms practice-based evidence. Mentors can then encourage reflection on the journey to date, coupled with encouraging the student to determine their next set of learning requirements within the placement.

Heutagogy will allow a student-centred take on the clinical experience activities that will contribute to personalizing, enriching and embedding learning beyond merely achieving an affirmative mark in their record. Students and mentors rightly make much of the need to meet the set clinical competency standards (Tiwari et al., 2005) but a responsibility surely exists to prepare students beyond the minimal exposure to experience benchmarks. Leading and facilitating the broadening of students' approaches to clinical learning can build motivation to learn, active and interactive student-centred learning capacity, self-directedness and enjoyment (Tiwari et al., 2006). Understanding what students feel about a placement's opportunities and their learning needs is therefore of some importance. It can underpin the direction of their learning in areas beyond mere competency at clinical tasks like seeing the family/patient perspective, ethical dimensions and comparing realties with their preconceived expectations (Cooper et al., 2005).

This can prove problematic in assessing student performance. There is often a dominant need for competences to be measured (McCarthy and Murphy, 2008). These are wider, and often highly specific to the individual learning outcomes, complicate this aspect of the mentor's leadership role further and call for astute judgements based upon the negotiated educational goal that was mutually agreed at the outset of placement.

Despite the complexities of the existing arena of practice-based education and introducing a new ethos of student-identified learning, we see heutagogy as being an approach of incremental or evolutionary improvement to the qualitative dimensions of student learning experiences in clinical contexts. Additionally, moving away from competency attainment as a solitary focus can embed transferrable skills in critical reflection; negotiation and leadership that enhance a journey towards graduateness and help students better assimilate theory to practice, ultimately benefiting patient care.

Mentorship barriers to heutagogy

Nurse education has a history of a pedagogic relationship between the teacher and the student, whether that is in the educational institution or the clinical area (Young and Paterson, 2007). While andragogy has been adopted in nurse education it still has connotations of a teacher–student relationship where it is always the teacher who decides what the student need to know and how the theory and skills (and in the nursing context their relationship to each other) should be taught (Dalley et al., 2008). In general, nurse education systems have traditionally assumed that learning has to be organized by others who make the appropriate associations and generalizations on behalf of the student. Nursing programmes rely on a curriculum that is usually approved by an academic board and has prescribed aims, objectives, content and assessment. Random individual experiences are therefore viewed as being totally inadequate sources of knowledge. This conflicts with the conceptualization of double-loop learning, which involves the challenging of the student's personal theories in use, their values and their assumptions, rather than simply reacting to a problem with strategies found in single-loop learning (Francis, 2004; Snelgrove, 2004).

The increasing complexity of modern nursing care delivery, the rapidly changing healthcare environment and the information explosion suggest the need for an educational approach in nursing where the students determine themselves what and how learning should take place. In these respects, heutagogy with this inherent emphasis upon self-identification of learning needs, in addition to a personal knowing of how to learn (as a fundamental skill) resonates as an important development, given the complexity of healthcare delivery environments. This is a challenge for the traditional concept of mentorship with its aforementioned unwritten curriculum of teacher-led rules. It also challenges the leadership attributes of the mentor in defending the right of the student to so fashion their learning and to step aside and allow the creation of educative experience that is prioritized differently from how they normally would.

Employability of nursing graduates and their perceived lack of clinical readiness has been a cause for concern (Clark and Holmes, 2007; NMC, 2007b). While skills gaps in nursing graduates are one aspect it is also argued that current academic approaches are inadequate and outdated. This is the case in the United Kingdom for example, despite nursing students' practice experience being half of the pre-registration nursing programme. It is one of the most important learning aspects of their educational preparation for entry into the profession with varied placements across clinical settings from the community to hospitals (Johns, 2005). Given this shared commitment to pre-registration preparation being embedded within practice, the role of the mentor as a teacher, supervisor and assessor is centrally important (especially where practice is such a large learning component): it is critical in helping to develop future generations of nurses.

Despite the magnitude (and provenance) in the United Kingdom of such relatively extensive student clinical exposure, evaluation of these experiences is variable and mentors remain uncertain about the effectiveness of promoting environments conducive to learning (Tremayne, 2007). Taylor (2008) notes the key role mentors have in the success of clinical placements, but cautions that the quality of mentorship in pre-registration is highly variable. Mentors have been criticized regarding their input into the educational experience of students and this can have a detrimental impact on skills development to deal with the unfolding diverse clinical situations (Nettleton and Bray, 2008), providing a potentially additional hurdle for the successful adoption of heutagogy.

It can be argued that mentor preparation conflicts with the standpoint of heutagogy, stemming from current guidelines and frameworks around the mentor role and training in which many parts are seen as being too prescriptive or inflexible for innovative student learning (Andrews and Chilton, 2000). This is substantiated by Watson (2000) and Elcock et al. (2007) who found that many mentors perceive their role in relation to student learning as being one of planning and structuring learning sessions. Furthermore, prescribing how learning and competency levels are achieved: the antithesis of heutagogy, thereby maintaining barriers to its ethos, ultimately leaving mentors to deem whether or not the student has achieved competence and a pass, but crucially not determined by their extant level of learning.

Breaking down the barriers

Rather than keeping student nurse learning in a linear model, the mentor adopting a heutagogical approach must strive to keep learning cyclical, with students exploring their own learning process, reacting to it and appraising the validity of what they studied. The main premise of this process emerges from the belief that mentors need to prepare students to be more proactive rather than reactive. In a heutagogical process the mentor steps back from the facilitator role – allowing students to question, foster and take the lead in their intellectual curiosities. The student must have time for reflective thinking, questioning theory, being critical of practice, exploration of their own values and attitudes plus truly engaging with the concept of heutagogy, all of which (as a package) can run contrary to traditional precepts and as such be discomforting for mentors.

Such a ground-shift in mentoring means they may need convincing regarding deconstructing the entire notion of pedagogy to make way for student ownership of learning. The primary mentor function thus becomes empowering students and providing resources only when asked. Mentors need to show leadership and relinquish their pedagogical role and commit to heutagogy, otherwise they will not effectively enable this innovation (Bray and Nettleton, 2007). Mentors need a desire to try something different, own such change and feel challenged by the prospect of working with students, rather than having students working for them (Myall et al., 2008). Spouse (1996) notes that mentors not fully committed to their role can impact negatively on student skills development. Heutagogy, when embraced by mentors, can truly acknowledge the importance of the learning experience and in developing life-long learning skills and values in student nurses, in which reflexivity and critical reflection are vital components of this suggested approach.

Recommendations for embedding heutagogy

Heutagogy within practice-based nurse education is an emergent rather than established learning approach. Its emergence from adult-based training and education fields is however arguably more of an evolutionary advance from andragogy and transformational learning, than a radical leap into the educative unknown. As such, the shift to heutagogical principles is about supporting the profession to understand and embrace the nuance and emphasis of the ethos to effect the transition. That notwithstanding, we accept that heutagogy provides challenges to educators and learners alike. Learner capability, a central tenet within heutagogy, has significant resonance with the aspirations of nurse education, further indicating mutual compatibility. This aspect requires the embedding within undergraduate, pre-registration curricula of critical and programmatic reflection to support and enhance student capacity to lead and shape their own learning. Central to that developmental need is advanced communications awareness and capabilities within students for them to suitably negotiate experiences and to articulate their learning.

Introducing this approach means a need for students having access to leadership knowledge and skills at an earlier stage and here assessing emotional intelligence may assist in selection and learning: an attribute potentially indicating improved attainment in nurse education (Rankin, 2011). Such an assay of student awareness capabilities may indicate ability to appreciate personal learning needs and potential to negotiate these fulsomely. It also means we explicitly acknowledge and revisit the philosophy and identity of nursing as being a combined technical, interpersonal, academic and clinical endeavour.

As discussed, developing mentor preparation to allow knowledge and awareness of the concept is also pivotal as to whether heutagogy becomes a dominant ethos within practice-based nurse education. This can be coupled with a greater commitment to link lecturer engagement in practice, enabling twin supports to not only embed the ethos but to develop and maintain an educational alignment and relationships between theory and practice, learners and teachers, universities and clinical placements and (most crucially) statutory learning requirements and individualized, self-determined learning experiences.

Heutagogy has the potential to transform clinical practice-based learning, providing an alternative view and construct of courses pertinent to each field of nursing. In many ways, when used as a framework to place around practice-based learning, heutagogy can help students unravel the ever-present and inherent uncertainties that define nursing practice.

References

Andrews, M. and Chilton, F. (2000), 'Student and mentor perceptions of mentoring effectiveness', *Nurse Education Today*, 20(7), 555–62.

Barron, D. and Hurley, J. (2012), 'Emotional intelligence and leadership', in J. Hurley and P. Linsley (eds), *Emotional Intelligence for the Health and Social Care Professional*. Oxford: Radcliffe Publishing.

Berragan, L. (2011), 'Simulation: an effective pedagogical approach for nursing?' *Nurse Education Today*, 31, 660–3.

Bray, L. and Nettleton, P. (2007), 'Assessor or mentor? Role confusion in professional education', *Nurse Education Today*, 27(8), 848–55.

Brown, L., Herd, K., Humphries, G. and Paton, M. (2005), 'The role of the lecturer in practice placements: what do students think?' *Nurse Education in Practice*, 5(2), 84–90.

Canning, N. (2010), 'Playing with heutagogy: exploring strategies to empower mature learners in higher education', *Journal of Further and Higher Education*, 34(1), 59–71.

Carper, B. A. (1978), 'Fundamental patterns of knowing in nursing', *Advances in Nursing Science*, 1(1), 13–24.

Carroll, P. (2006), *Nursing Leadership and Management: A Practical Guide*. New York: Thomson Delmar Learning.

Clark, T. and Holmes, S. (2007), 'Fit for practice? An exploration of the development of newly qualified nurses using focus groups', *International Journal of Nursing Studies*, 44(7), 1210–20.

Cooper, C., Taft, L. B. and Thelen, M. (2005), 'Preparing for practice: students' reflections on their final clinical experience', *Journal of Professional Nursing*, 21(5), 293–302.

Cowan, D. T., Norman, I. and Coopamah, V. P. (2005), 'Competence in nursing practice: a controversial concept – a focused review of literature', *Nurse Education Today*, 25, 355–62.

Dalley, L., Candela, J. and Benzel-Lindley, J. (2008), 'Learning to let go: the challenge of de-crowding the curriculum', *Nurse Education Today*, 28(1), 62–9.

Elcock, K., Curtis, P. and Sharples, K. (2007), 'Supernumerary status: an unrealised ideal', *Nurse Education in Practice*, 7(1), 4–10.

Francis, D. (2004), 'Reconstructing the meaning given to critical incidents in nurse education', *Nurse Education in Practice*, 4(4), 244–9.

Franks, V. (2004), 'Evidence-based uncertainty in mental health nursing', *Journal of Psychiatric and Mental Health Nursing*, 11, 99–105.

Glover, D., Law, S. and Youngman, A. (2002), 'Graduateness and employability: student perceptions of the personal outcomes of university education', *Research in Post-Compulsory Education*, 7(3), 293–6.

Hase, S. and Kenyon, C. (2000), 'From andragogy to heutagogy', *Ultibase, Royal Melbourne Institute of Technology*, December.

Hurley, J., Angking, D., Burnip, S., Colgrave, J., Cutler, K., Smith, K. and Wicken, M. (2012), 'Preparing undergraduate nurses for leadership: from communication theory for clinical practice', in R.Vanderzwan (ed.), *Current Trends in Technology and Society*, Volume 1. Brisbane: Primrose Hall Publishing.

Johns, R. (2005), 'Prioritising to safeguard the integrity of nurse education', *Nursing Times*, 101(34), 26.

McCarthy, B. and Murphy, S. (2008), 'Assessing undergraduate nursing students in clinical practice: do preceptors use assessment strategies?' *Nurse Education Today*, 28, 301–13.

Myall, M., Levett-Jones, T. and Lathlean, J. (2008), 'Mentorship in contemporary practice: the experiences of nursing students and practice mentors', *Journal of Clinical Nursing*, 17(14), 1834–42.

Nettleton, P. and Bray, L. (2008), 'Current mentorship schemes might be doing our students a disservice', *Nurse Education in Practice*, 8(3), 205–12.

Northington, L., Wilkerson, R., Fisher, W. and Schenk, L. (2005), 'Enhancing nursing students' clinical experiences using aesthetics', *Journal of Professional Nursing*, 21(1), 66–71.

Nursing and Midwifery Council (NMC) (2002), *Supporting Nurses and Midwives Through Lifelong Learning*. London: NMC.

— (2007a), *Simulation and Practice Learning Project: Outcome of a Pilot Study to Test the Principles for Auditing Simulated Practice Learning Environments in the Pre-registration Nursing Programme (Final Report)*. London: NMC.

— (2007b), *The Future of Pre-registration Nursing Education – NMC Consultation*. London: NMC.

Owen, S., Ferguson, K. and Baguley, I. (2005), 'The clinical activity of mental health nurse lecturers', *Journal of Psychiatric and Mental Health Nursing*, 12(3), 310–16.

Paterson, K., Henderson, A. and Trivella, A. (2010), 'Educating for leadership: a programme designed to build a responsive health care culture', *Journal of Nursing Management*, 18, 78–83.

Rankin, R. F. (2011), *Emotional Intelligence: Attrition and Attainment in Nursing and Midwifery Education*. Berlin: Lambert Academic Publishing.

Scottish Executive Health Department (SEHD) (2006), *Modernising Nursing Careers: Setting the Direction*. Edinburgh: Scottish Executive.

Snelgrove, S. (2004), 'Approaches to learning of student nurses', *Nurse Education Today*, 24(8), 605–14.

Spouse, J. (1996), 'The effective mentor: a model for student-centred learning', *Nursing Times*, 92, 120–33.

Stanley, D. and Sherratt, A. (2010), 'Lamp light on leadership: clinical leadership and Florence Nightingale', *Journal of Nursing Management*, 18(2), 115–21.

Taylor, J. (2008), 'Are you a good mentor?' *Nursing Times*, 104(32), 18–20.

Tiwari, A., Lam, D., Yeun, K. H., Chan, R., Fung, T. and Chan S. (2005), 'Student learning in clinical nursing education: perceptions between assessment and learning', *Nurse Education Today*, 25, 299–308.

Tiwari, A., Chan, S., Wong, E., Wong, D., Chui, C., Wong, A. and Patil, N. (2006), 'The effects of problem-based learning on students' approaches to learning in the context of clinical nursing education', *Nurse Education Today*, 26, 430–8.

Tremayne, P. (2007), 'Improving clinical placements through evaluation and feedback to staff', *Nursing Times*, 103(25), 32–3.

Watson, S. (2000), 'The support that mentors receive in the clinical setting', *Nurse Education Today*, 20(7), 585–92.

Young, L. and Paterson, B. (2007), *Teaching Nursing: Developing a Student-centred Learning Environment*. Philadelphia: Lippincott Williams and Wilkins.

7

The Learner's Perspective

Barbara A. Brandt

Summary

In this chapter I present the findings of a research project examining adult student perspectives on the use of heutagogically derived learning methods in an online course. I relate my personal reflections, including the transformational learning experience of temporarily adopting an 'alter ego', and the real-time contributions from an expert in the field. Small group discussions elicited the theme of positive evaluation of our instructor and this was confirmed by subsequent research. A phenomenological inquiry of the adult students was conducted. Thoughts and feeling from the participants in this research were collected using an online questionnaire. The development of interpersonal relationships between students and with the instructor, and the use of student posts and reading as resources for learning experiences were an integral part of the application of heutagogy. Also important was the encouragement of individual exploration which was enhanced by group discovery. All of these factors combined to make effective use of the e-learning environment. Students indicated a strong preference for self-determined learning.

Introduction to heutagogy in online class

During an elective, online course, I was exposed to the term 'heutagogy', a word new to my lexicon. This graduate-level class was intense; it compressed a 15-week education course into a four-week summer session. It encompassed an overview of the principles of adult education, with opportunities to choose topics and delve into them more thoroughly. As one of the few master of education students in a class composed primarily of doctoral candidates, I quickly discovered I was, 'under-knowledged'. My classmates included fellow educators, ranging from elementary school to high school to university levels, and in academic fields ranging from general education, to sports, to sciences and to music. Other classmates worked in human services and administrative areas. The online posts involved in-depth discussions of readings and personal experiences, with thoughtful questions and challenges posed between participants and course leader. The educational terminology and references used were completely quite new to me. So, in the beginning, I found myself looking up vocabulary and concept definitions, authors and articles for almost every sentence I read. I felt like I was climbing a mountain of knowledge. It was tough but exhilarating.

Our professor provided lists of resources to read and discuss, some required and some optional, and also encouraged us to explore resources in our interest areas. In the first two weeks, two readings about heutagogy were provided and discussed. Halfway through the course, the professor solicited input as to how the course was going and if it was meeting our needs and what changes might be made. Class time was provided for critical self-reflection. The final assessment was a project of our choice with the professor presenting a variety of ideas but with the option of allowing us to propose and negotiate our own project. The course followed many of the heutagogical principles that I had read about and which are described in detail in Chapter 1 of this book.

Heutagogy in action, personal narrative of the 'alter ego'

A classmate emailed Stewart Hase to discover the correct pronunciation and derivation of heutagogy. Her initiative, his response and the course professor asking the class to delve into the thoughts of noted educational scholars, led me to dare to experiment with the idea of adopting a temporary 'alter ego' and looking through their eyes at what we were learning.

On the web, I researched authors from three of our readings: Stewart Hase, Edward Taylor and Ian Baptiste. I discovered the universities with which they were associated and their areas of interest in research and teaching. I determined their viewpoints on educational theories and profiled their personal traits. I role played each author in my small group discussions, writing as though I were each person, using their words, with my interpretations of what they might say, and signing the posts using first names. My classmates responded to the remarks, asking each 'alter ego' questions to clarify and elicit additional information. As the discussion continued and I reviewed theories espoused in other articles, I found myself thinking, 'Oh, this is what Ian would say', and 'Stewart would agree with this'. I started to see the authors as real people, rather than authors, which helped to organize the educational theories in my mind. I concluded that my ability to understand increased when I personally related with the authors and their ideas. As an independent learner, I was able to '. . . recognize the learning moment' (Hase, 2009, p. 45). I did not know this about myself, previously, it was a transformative experience.

Posing as Edward, I reviewed transformative learning theory. As Stewart, I considered people watching, personal contact, mindfulness and use of technology. Since Stewart is from Australia, I mentioned having a vegemite sandwich, though I do not know if this is actually on his menu. While responding to a classmate's question on the use of technology for civic engagement, I decided Stewart would say that, 'I find myself in agreement with Ian Baptiste, who believes civic engagement takes place best at the local level.' Then, I had Stewart invite Ian to join the conversation. As Ian, I commented on computer usage by a doctoral student in a community energy programme (Rushton, 2005).

I emailed Stewart, described the role-playing activity and provided copies of the posts where I played his alter ego. I asked if he would be willing to participate and submitted a list of questions for him to consider. When I told my son, a graduate student in natural science, what I was doing, he was incredulous. He asked how I dared to write to a leader in the field and why I actually let that person know what I was doing in class. I told him one of the advantages of getting older is that you discover that it really doesn't matter. What is the worst that could happen? Stewart could say no or not reply. Since I did receive a reply, along with Stewart's participation in the class activity, my son learned that it is permissible to step outside school rules and regulations and try something new.

Stewart replied that he was, 'enjoying this bit of informal e-learning with you'. He sent an informational email on understanding learning, the role of emotions in learning and educational experiences. He answered questions on educational systems, technology and the use of the web. I appreciated the reference to his personal life and his comment that, 'The implications for how we understand learning are interesting. If I were a graduate student now starting a research program, rather than being at the other end of my working life, I'd be examining the role of emotions in learning and the role neuropsychological factors have in what is clearly a complex process' (email response, Hase, 2011). I posted his reply in the discussion group, making it clear that, this time, the words were from Stewart Hase, himself. The students in the class were impressed with his response and with receiving first-hand remarks. Interchange with a leader in the field of heutagogy, through a web-based course, confirmed that, 'E-learning enables access to the most contemporary information, delivered by professionals regarded as experts in their fields' (Ashton and Elliott, 2007, p. 170).

The week after the alter ego activity, when I wanted to delve further into heutagogy and action research, the professor suggested that I spend the entire next week on that topic and ignore the readings. I was not sure what to think of this at first. I wondered if I could trust that it was acceptable to skip the readings and study my interest area. Canning (2010) found that students beginning studies employing heutagogical principles had concerns when given this sort of freedom including completing assignments correctly, being supported in their efforts and wanting to achieve. I absolutely agreed with these findings!

I learned how to 'do' school at a young age. Find out what the teacher wants, do it and reap the reward of good grades. The same formula worked in college. I spent time discovering how the instructor wants things completed, did it and then earned the good grades. Shor (1992, p. 18) described these traditional educational experiences as ones that, '. . . transfer facts, skills, or values without meaningful connection to their (students) needs, interest, or community cultures'. The learning that I really wanted to do, I did on my own time. I did not consider the possibility of getting university credits for self-selected learning activities.

I was sceptical when the professor encouraged us to use self-determined learning. I questioned how grades could be assigned. However, when I was given the information and support I required, I came to the realization that I could use my learning to earn university credits. I felt almost excited. I believed I could trust the negotiation process of reading and assessment as it related to the use of heutagogy (Hase and Kenyon, 2000). As explained by Kenyon and Hase (2001, p. 296), 'Assessment becomes more of a learning experience rather than a means to measure attainment.' I stepped out of my school comfort zone and entered into my outside-of-school learning mode. I observed and joined in as we students chose our topics of interest, did our research or activity, and reported back to the class. I relished the interchange among the disciplines, as we discussed each others' areas. My knowledge increased, in my area and in theirs, as I caught fellow students' passion for the topics.

After the course: Personal reflection on heutagogy

It was difficult to return to regular online classes, after having had the experience of being able to actively participate in the selection of my learning topics and activities in the summer course. I felt frustrated and forced when I had to read the articles the teachers selected, with little room for my own interest areas. It was hard to return to the way I had 'done' school for so long. Some teachers gave options in choices from a list of topics and that helped. Having tasted the freedom of learning and getting the benefit of university credit for it, I wanted more. I wanted to write to the instructors and relate my ideas and tell them where I needed new knowledge. The years of disciplined obedience kept me quiet – grades are important, after all.

The next year, I took an online class on diversity and I knew the students in my class: we came from diverse backgrounds. I read the objectives for the class and got excited about what we could learn from each other, about each others' cultures and lifestyles. I couldn't wait to start asking my classmates questions but was nervous about sharing information about myself. However, I trusted the other students and remembered the considerable personal growth that stepping out of my comfort zone had previously brought me. Then, the course began. There was no time for bringing out additional topics. There were too many articles and videos assigned to read and watch. The discussions were frequently stilted and often boring. We were required to read from Wikipedia frequently; although I do use Wikipedia for recreational reading, as a mathematician I do not value it for graduate work. I tried to fit in time to read the original source articles, instead of relying on Wikipedia, but it was hard to keep up with the amount of work required. I had to force myself to do the assignments, some of them similar to high school worksheets designed to see if one had read the material. I did acquire knowledge in the class. I did learn. The problem for me was that I wanted to be far more actively involved in my learning as I had been on my previous course.

For a while, I wished I had never had the chance to use heutagogy in an online university environment at all, then I wouldn't be missing it as much as I was. Upon reflection, the opportunity to self-direct my learning that summer (in school, as I also usually do in life), was an incredible experience: one I wanted to repeat.

Process of beginning research

When Stewart invited our adult education class to write a chapter about their experience with heutagogy in a new book he was editing with Chris Kenyon, three of us met in a small group, online, to discuss heutagogy, its meaning and its potentials for research. We had differing viewpoints on the application and role of heutagogy in our online class. We proposed a variety of research types. One area in which we did come to an agreement was the positive evaluation of the teacher/ instructor. One student related how the instructor gave private encouragement in emails to students. Another student felt the support of the professor in and out of class was important. I spoke about how the professor had dealt with my concerns about how grades worked, when applying heutagogy in class.

I decided to conduct research to determine which areas would be of importance to my classmates. It would also be interesting to see what other themes would appear, as input from more students was collected. I wanted to see how the class felt about the value of the instructor.

Method

This phenomenological study investigated student experiences of being exposed to heutagogical principles in an online learning environment. It sought to identify applications of heutagogy and to examine the effects of the use of self-determined learning on relationships between learner/classmates/instructor, lessons learned and emotions of the students. Data was collected using an online questionnaire.

Twelve students enrolled in an online course on adult education were invited to participate. As a student in that online course, I had access to fellow students. Students received an email invitation to participate, including a link to the survey/interview and an explanation of the purpose of the research. One follow-up email was sent as a reminder/second invitation. Completing the survey/ interview was understood as giving consent to participate. All participants were assured of confidentiality and anonymity.

Results

Six students agreed to participate. General themes were identified, and responses were compiled.

During analysis, five general themes emerged. (1) The participants identified heutagogical principles used in their online course. Resources for learning experiences included choices of topics and readings, student-led asynchronous discussions and the instructor as a facilitator. (2) A positive valuation of the teacher, with the highest regard in the area of encouragement provided. (3) Relationship development between classmates resulted in a supportive atmosphere where clarifying questions and challenging or motivating comments led to increased discoveries. (4) Respondents felt self-determined learning was important and indicated it as their personal preference for its use in their own education. (5) Participants applied heutagogical principles to other aspects of their lives, including as teachers and as learners.

The first survey question was: 'Heutagogy is self-determined learning. When did you first hear the term "heutagogy"? What were your initial thoughts?'

One participant, who submitted an incomplete survey, with only this first question answered, stated, 'I have never heard about it before.' Since, as noted in the introduction, all students were required to read and discuss two articles on heutagogy, this answer serves as evidence of Carl Rogers' hypothesis that, 'We cannot teach another person directly: we can only facilitate learning' (Hase and Kenyon, 2000, p. 295). Although this student had read and commented on the topic of heutagogy, the student did not retain any memory of it. The student did not even recall that heutagogy had been a part of the course.

Four participants first heard of heutagogy in their online classes, just as I did. One felt it was a, 'Big word for something that is done all the time.' Another thought it was a, 'Fancy name' but 'Framed what to do on a weekly basis with my students.' Two compared it to, 'a sub-category of andragogy' or 'just another "-gogy" someone made up to have something novel (sic) to publish about.' Another participant, who instructs pre-service teachers, 'Identified heutagogy with much of my teaching practice.' This student thought about the amount of, 'Teacher-directed versus learner-directed' coursework, and wondered, 'how much my future teachers will consider these processes in their future classrooms'. The student considered their own learning, also, bringing up the idea of where authority or power lies, 'I react differently when the power structures in a class change, how I'm self-directed in my private life and how education can both make that possible and also squelch those opportunities for students.'

Questions 2 to 7 dealt with the online course the participants took, 'How were heutagogical principles integrated in this online course?'

Key words in the responses for the second question included readings, interest, selection and topics. The participants noted, 'Self-selection of certain readings and topics of interest', 'Choice of learning topics' and 'Select an aspect of adult education that was of personal interest . . . or switch to another option of their choosing'. The use of, 'Discussion posts to analyze and interpret readings' and 'Threaded discussions' were mentioned as means of sharing information among classmates. One participant mentioned the professor, who was available for guidance 'If needed'. The student wrote, 'Throughout the process the instructor happily adjusted and encouraged others to explore their own interests as long as they were generally fitting in with the context of the course'. Another participant felt heutagogical principles were, 'a guiding principle of the course'.

Question 3: 'How did you apply self-determined learning to the course?'

Application included the process of selection and research of topics, posting in discussions and considering various implications. One participant said, 'I apply self-determined learning to everything and choose what I think is most relevant to my goals'. Another stated that, 'It was my modus operandi'. Another one said 'I took advantage of the opportunity to "get credit" for the explorations I did outside of the assigned readings and discussions'. I related to this comment. Getting university credit for learning something I wanted to study was one of the benefits of the use of heutagogy.

Question 4: 'What role did the instructor have in your use of self-determined learning?'

Analysis of the responses to the fourth question brought out words including 'encouraged, open, discussion, and explorations'. Only positive comments appeared in the answers to this question. Over half of the participants remarked on the encouragement provided by the professor. When considering the role of the instructor, subjects wrote, 'Encouraged us to determine our own learning paths . . . engaged in discussion with us about our explorations' and 'Encouraged us to be creative, to go exploring'. This shows agreement with the positive valuation of the teacher, regarding encouragement provided, first discovered in small group discussions, previously mentioned.

The idea of facilitation and guidance emerged from the responses. One student mentioned having the same instructor in previous courses and, 'Understanding the facilitating approach for a social constructivist style of teaching', both areas which had arisen in our small group discussions. Another participant, who felt the professor was, 'Absolutely wonderful and open as a guide', discussed the idea of guidance in heutagogy with, 'In this case (the teacher) continually suggested options and direction to consider while always leaving a door open which you, as the learner, could venture through if you so chose, one (the teacher) would be excited to learn about'. A teacher using a flexible curriculum, ". . . changes from lecturer or instructor to facilitator and coach' (Hase, 2009, p. 47).

One student mentioned trust issues and wrote, 'It's too easy to "follow the rules' sometimes, but having known (the professor) in the past it made it easy to trust (him) and know that this self-determined learning was truly acceptable.' This brought out a third area from our small group discussion; having trust was important for a positive valuation of the teacher.

Question 5: 'What role did your classmates have in your use of self-determined learning?"

Here, common words and phrases included 'questions, asked, self-determined, information, personal, learning, and pushed me'. Classmates asked questions, provided support and taught each other. As related by one student, classmates asked questions, 'seeking clarification or leading me down a different path . . . they pushed me to personally explore further (self-determined) by choosing to respond to some and not to others, to hunt for additional resources and go down rabbit-holes before generating a response or simply tucking the information away for my own personal learning'. 'The students in the class . . . weren't afraid to ask questions, to challenge ideas, and that pushed me to carefully reconsider what I know/think/feel, consider why, and search out new information as necessary.' One student felt classmates, 'Were inspirational . . . I remember being interested in and motivated by all the different things they were reading and how they were processing the readings in their own minds.' Another participant replied that classmates, 'Supported my statements and asked clarifying questions, but my use of self-determined learning was still a personal experience.'

Question 6: 'What were your experiences/lessons learned through the use of heutagogy?'

Variations on the word 'learn', along with 'freedom, choosing, and power', were top word responses to this question. Participants focused on the concept of learning. One student although 'willing to be exposed to multiple forms of information', wanted 'to direct my own learning path'. One participant questioned what lessons may have been learned, 'Heutagogy seems to be just another term for lifelong learning or informal learning . . . . and I don't think I could list anymore what the principles of heutagogy are.' This inability to recall the principles is a second reinforcement of Roger's hypothesis about student-centred learning.

Another participant reflected on conflict over the ages of students who can apply heutagogy:

I've learned one of the most important takeaways I have from the course is a disagreement over whether or not heutagogy is solely for adult learners. I do not believe that it is. When students are given a choice over what it is they are to read or research, when students are presented with required learning targets and are given the freedom to demonstrate proficient understanding of these essential concepts in a way of their own choosing, etc. then heutagogy is in play. This isn't a concept reserved for those whose brains have reached physical maturation (our pedagogy/andragogy 'cut-off') but is applicable at all stages of life and open to all learners.

This student went on to discuss the concepts of freedom and power.

> I appreciate the freedom that (the teacher) presented to us as adult learners, and realize more than ever that these issues are really more about power than anything else. The power of the instructor to decide the rules of the game, requires that 'knowledge' be presented in a pre-selected form/intelligence of the teacher's choosing, etc. 'The student applies this personally by reflecting on being a teacher and seeing a need to increase applications of heutagogy.' Recognizing that I already integrate heutagogy into my classes was a good lesson, though I also realized my need to further push the envelope to let my students truly determine the direction that their learning will go.

Question 7: 'How did you feel about the inclusion/use of self-determined learning in the course?'

In contrast to a comment made in question 2, where a participant felt heutagogical principles were, 'A guiding principle of the course', one student felt that, 'Although the use of heutagogy was satisfactory, there were aspects of adult learning that were much more dominant in this course than heutagogy.' Two students felt its use to be important in adult education. Three participants felt positive about the inclusion. One said, 'LOVE IT!' Another said that, 'It's essential.' One student felt it was necessary to have regular assignments:

> I liked it that the instructor encouraged us in this way in addition to, as opposed to instead of, our regular class assignments, because it would be difficult in an online course to just have everyone doing their own explorations and somehow try to have a meaningful class discussion.

Question 8: 'How have you used/applied heutagogical principles in other courses/situations?'

The same student who did not recall heutagogical principles, stated that, 'I'm constantly aware of my learning how to learn, especially in the workplace.... I'm not sure whether I'm employing them (heutagogical principles) or not.'

One student said that he or she had used applications while teaching, 'I have encouraged my own students to become more involved in their own learning processes.' Another had applied heutagogical principles in a multitude of situations, while teaching and while learning, saying that there were,

> Too many (uses) to mention. Being deep into my dissertation I've obviously been a self-directed learner as I've chosen a topic, sifted through the literature base, decided what to present and how to categorize and organize it, viewed other dissertations as examples to replicate, etc. I've also rearranged any number of aspects of the courses that I teach. Students now have much more freedom over some of the topics of their presentations and the ways in which they choose to present.

Question 9: 'Please add any additional information/views on heutagogy. For example, you might wish to provide a narrative about your heutagogical experiences in the course.'

One student chose to respond to this final question and wanted to promote the earlier use of heutagogy, due to our fast-paced and fast-changing world:

> I think that heutagogy isn't age-specific but is rather much more related to roles of power and the ways in which younger students are often subjected to the will of the teacher. Although this potentially lessens with time, plenty of power situations and teacher-directed (as opposed to teacher-guided) learning still characterize American education . . . Heutagogy is key to democratic society and should be introduced/fostered early on in education so that, as students mature, they're used to taking initiative for their own learning and are seeking out information and applying it in creative ways . . . Our world changes so quick; we, as citizens of the world, don't know what tomorrow, much less next week, next year or future decades will look like. Applying heutagogical principles throughout the education system most importantly teaches students to learn, to question, to seek out, to synthesize, to apply to their personal context, etc. It, and these skills, are critical if we're to prepare learners for an unknown and unpredictable world.

Ashton and Newman (2006, p. 829) address the issue of balance of power in the classroom, emphasizing that capabilities must be developed, along with skills and knowledge; to accomplish this, teachers 'must relinquish some power'.

Conclusions

Hybrid or blended learning, which includes face-to-face and online class contact, has the potential to integrate the existing world with the classroom.

Virtual connections, made through the internet, can provide opportunities for real-time input from experts in the field of study. Ashton and Newman (2006, p. 826) consider this as, 'rational for flexible and blended delivery'. The narrative aspect of this chapter depicted a student experience in an online course, where a connection was made with an expert in the field of heutagogy, resulting in the expansion of individual and class knowledge in the area. This connection continued with an invitation to conduct research and write a chapter for this book, intertwining educational experiences in the United States with research from international authors.

The implication of this collaboration is far reaching. Imagine every university course making provisions for students to access top minds in their fields of study. With internet access available in schools, students could be encouraged to seek real-time input from these experts and consider this as being similar to bringing in guest speakers, not just from the local region, but from around the world. It would be left to the experts in the field to determine the amount of time they are willing and able to spend in this form of student consultation. Mentoring, research collaboration and international connections are possible, positive benefits of this heutagogical application in online, or hybrid, courses.

While discussing the integration of heutagogical applications into a teacher education programme, Canning (2010) noted that emotional energy comes into play. Students learn how to co-construct knowledge through the use of scaffolding questions and comments from each other and from the instructor. The teacher/instructor needs to provide encouragement and support throughout the process of the students' learning how to self-direct their studies. The research indicates that the teacher is valuable and important to each student's progress in self-determined learning.

This finding implies a necessary change in the role of the instructor from leader to guide or facilitator. Hase (2009) describes this change as a move from teacher to facilitator and coach. Since meeting curriculum requirements is part of the instructor's responsibilities, there may be some required topics or required readings in the course. These curriculum mandates may need to be altered, as we transform learning from a traditional approach to a self-determined approach. Teachers remain a foundational part of the classroom, providing encouragement, support, inspiration and resource suggestions while serving as a resource themselves.

During my course, I noted that students were able to be open with each other when they asked clarifying questions, challenged developing ideas, supported statements and presented the results from their own studies. The asynchronous online posts were extensive in length and reflected considerable depth of thought. It was a safe place, where I could explore and share my interests. The research showed that a good relationship between classmates created a supportive atmosphere. This further implies the need to create a safe environment, where students will feel encouraged to participate in the exchange of ideas. In hybrid courses, a face-to-face meeting may be used to make connections between classmates. In online courses, a beginning session of introductions can serve as a way of increasing the level of comfort with the different approach. Canning's introducing programme (2010, p. 62) used, 'standard things like form filling and getting to know you activities'.

Shor (1992) promotes empowering education as a path to critical learning and democratic discourse. He defines it as, 'a student-centered program for multicultural democracy in school and society' (p. 15). I see heutagogy as a form of empowering education. The students' self-determined studies lead to transformational experiences; this benefits individual learners and ultimately society. The participants in this small study reported applying heutagogical principles to other aspects of their lives, including as teachers and as learners. This result suggests strongly that there is a need to incorporate heutagogy into more educational experiences.

When I teach a workshop on the use of manipulative materials in mathematics, my goal is for attendees to return to their classrooms and incorporate at least one new manipulative material, in at least one lesson. Manipulative materials are three-dimensional objects, which the students move or manipulate in order to demonstrate and develop mathematical concepts. A pre-school teacher might have the school purchase coloured plastic tiles for students to create or copy patterns, such as red tile, blue tile, red tile, blue tile. A third grade teacher might use everyday objects to teach division, start with 32 lima beans, put them into 4 paper cups, evenly, and discover 8 beans will be in each cup. An algebra teacher, with a purchased set of plastic cubes, sticks and flats representing base ten, could have the students demonstrate algebraic multiplication, starting with the stick representing the number ten and leading to the stick representing the variable 'x'. Step by step, as the instructors incorporate additional manipulative materials into a wider variety of lessons, they increase their abilities in the area of teaching math using concrete materials. The students increase their understanding of math concepts.

In my research for this chapter, the participants identified aspects of heutagogical applications, felt heutagogical experiences were important and preferred to learn using self-determined experiences. This leads to one last, main implication. We need to increase instructors' abilities in the area of teaching using heutagogical applications. As educators teach other educators, they can model heutagogical principles. Educators can be encouraged to incorporate at least one heutagogical application, in at least one course. A teacher might let their students select their topic for one assignment, providing a list of possibilities for the students who need guidance in their choice. The teacher may allow their students to choose their method of presentation, including essays, plays, poetry, art, music and computer applications. Grades might become a process of negotiation, between the student and the teacher. Step by step, as the instructors incorporate heutagogical principles into their classes, they go through the process of changing their role, from leader to guide. They allow their students to become self-determined learners. The students will thank them for this.

Acknowledgements

I would like to extend a sincere thank you to: Dr Frank A. Guldbrandsen, Academic Advisor for this project, for his willingness to assist a first-time researcher; Michael R. Reichenbach and Ann Fandrey, fellow classmates in the adult education course, for their participation in small group discussions on heutagogy and research.

References

Ashton, J. and Elliott, R. (2007), 'Juggling the balls: study, work, family and play: student perspectives on flexible and blended heutagogy', *European Early Childhood Education Research Journal*, 15(2), 167–81.

Ashton, J. and Newman, L. (2006), 'An unfinished symphony: 21st century teacher education using knowledge creating heutagogies', *British Journal of Educational Technology*, 37, 825–40.

Canning, N. (2010). 'Playing with heutagogy: exploring strategies to empower mature learners in higher education', *Journal of Further and Higher Education*, 34(1), 59–71.

Hase, S. (2009), 'Heutagogy and e-learning in the workplace: some challenges and opportunities', *Impact: Journal of Applied Research in Workplace E-Learning*, 1(1), 43–52.

—. (2011), Email sent to Barbara Brandt, Sunday, 17 July.

Hase, S. and Kenyon, C. (2000), 'From andragogy to heutagogy', *Ultibase*, RMIT, December. Retrieved 8 November 2012 from: www.psy.gla.ac.uk/~steve/pr/ Heutagogy.html.

Kenyon, C. and Hase, S. (2001), 'Moving from andragogy to heutagogy in vocational education', in *Research to Reality: Putting VET Research to Work, Proceedings of the Australian Vocational Education and Training Research Association (AVETRA) Conference*, 28–30 March, Adelaide.

Rushton, G. (2005), 'Civic engagement in Philadelphia, Grenada', PennState Live, University of Penn State. Posted 22 December at: http://live.psu.edu/story/15225.

Shor, I. (1992), *Empowering Education*. London: University of Chicago Press.

Part Three

Heutagogy in the Wider Education World

8

Developing Creativity

Fred Garnett

Summary

This chapter analyses The Beatles music making in the 1960s using the Open Context Model of Learning (Luckin et al., 2010) to identify the learning processes they went through and how those processes affected their music. The purpose of this is to try and uncover what underlies their enduring creativity and how this informs the process of learning and, in particular, heutagogy. The Open Context Model of Learning is concerned with examining how the education process itself might be structured to enable more creativity to emerge naturally, within learning, rather than being a thing apart, uncovered in various cultural contexts outside of formal education.

The Beatles themselves, 'four underachieving schoolboys' who 'changed the world' (Riley, 2002), seem ideal subjects for such an analysis of how you might learn to be creative. There are useful lessons to be drawn out from this analysis, most notably that the creative phase of learning is deeply rooted in building meaningful collaborations. In this chapter we will look at how The Beatles recorded work reveals such learning to us because, as Gruber (1989) says, creativity is 'developmental and systemic: it happens in stages over the course of a lifetime'. What follows is one way of representing those stages.

Open Context Model of Learning

The Open Context Model of Learning posits three phases of learning across the PAH (pedagogic-andragogic-heutagogic) Continuum:

Pedagogic: when we learn using the focus of a subject discipline to structure that learning; for The Beatles their chosen subject was 'hit records'.
Andragogic: when we learn how to negotiate what we want to learn both within and beyond a subject discipline, and how to collaborate with others in the social processes of learning.
Heutagogic: when we begin to understand what the structure and form of our subject is and how we can start to play with form and transform it.

So the Open Context Model pre-supposes that we not only need to understand the structures of the subject under study, but also that we need to both identify processes of collaboration as well as strategies for creative renewal. Fortunately for this analysis George Martin, who signed The Beatles to his record label Parlophone in 1962, explicitly uses educational analogies in discussing their working together in 'All You Need is Ears' (2001). He observes that he was 'like a schoolteacher' in the early days (1962–4) (pedagogy), and that after recording 'Yesterday' (June 1965) they became collaborators (andragogy), reflecting the first two stages of the PAH Continuum.

The Beatles and the Open Context Model of Learning

I intend to argue that we could map these three phases of learning to three phases of Beatles recorded music. I am not covering the creative play of their childhood like Glassman, nor their evolution from The Quarrymen in 1957 as Gladwell (2008) does in 'Outliers'. In fact, for reasons discussed below the Open Context Model phase of The Beatles' own learning process as creative musicians ended when they recorded 'I Am The Walrus' in September 1967 (Lewisohn, 2010) and was then followed by two further phases, not discussed here, the self-managed Apple period, 1968, and their collapse in 1969.

Phase 1: 1962–4

Pedagogic excellence; from the parlour to the scream

This first phase of The Beatles learning concerns the time they focused on writing and recording 'hit records'. The music industry in England in the early

1960s treated pop music as a 'here today, gone tomorrow' concern where the artists were seen as disposable. The smart ones, like early 'rocker' Tommy Steele aimed to be all round family entertainers (Frame, 2007). The real money-spinners for the music industry before The Beatles were soundtrack albums: for five years in the 1960s soundtracks were the biggest selling albums. In an irony that he must have lived with ever since, Cliff Richard finally hit gold dust with this formula with his soundtrack for Summer Holiday in the very week that The Beatles 'Please Please Me' went to number one in the United Kingdom, February 1963, and changed the rules of the 'hit record' game. 'Please Please Me' was significant for any number of reasons but here are two. The Beatles refused to record potential 'hit records' written by other songwriters and George Martin; in George's words the 'school master' of his studio, reshaped the 1 minute and 10 seconds of 'Please Please Me' that The Beatles finally offered him, into the signature sound of Mersey Beat. This incorporated the harmonica-driven rising chords, the excitement of McCartney's 'I, Me, You' lyrics (Miles, 1998) embedded in the music as the group ensemble performance of a rock song: right through your feet and direct to your heart. The rest of 1963 saw the consolidation of that style and it became the new formula for hit records during 1963 and 1964 in the United Kingdom.

The massive success of their self-penned 'hit record' meant they needed to put an album together to capitalize on its success. George Martin, clearly in charge of directing The Beatles musically in early 1963, astutely decided that their first album would be a version of the stage act that had made their name. The workaholic Beatles played live concerts relentlessly throughout 1963 and a 'fan souvenir' album not only made sense when albums were rare and expensive commodities, but tied in with the prevailing notion of albums being soundtracks.

Refining the subject; 'With The Beatles'

Their second album, 'With The Beatles', released in November 1963, consolidated the framework of the first album. Tuomas Eerola identifies it as demonstrating the 'uniform traits' of the Mersey Beat style. They used the framework of their live act caught in the studio but upped their game by writing several new songs. Significantly, the first five songs are all Lennon and McCartney originals and the album instantly became the biggest selling record of 1963. While this was a better-recorded album, it didn't represent any development musically. Rather, it reprised the first album with more care and attention. Culturally, however, it was a massive event, coming after the media-baptized birth of Beatlemania and a Royal Variety Performance. This marked the beginning of Beatles releases being cultural events dominating the media landscape in the United Kingdom. While 'With The Beatles' did not represent a musical or a creative advance on 'Please Please Me', it did contain the track 'I Wanna Be Your Man', that gave their friends, the Rolling Stones, their own breakthrough. The Beatles' own globally most significant single 'I Want To Hold Your Hand', was released a week later and was not on the 'With The Beatles' album.

So three key tropes of The Beatles' musical activity, classic singles, great albums and support of fellow artists, were fully in place by November 1963. It was shortly followed by a fourth trope, dominating the British Christmas, when albums were more likely to be bought as presents. A fifth trope, multimedia production, emerged when BBC TV launched 'Top of The Pops' on 2 January 1964. However, most of the events between 13 October 1963 and 2 January 1964 represented the growth of the social phenomenon of Beatlemania rather than the evolution off their musical abilities.

Between March and June 1964 The Beatles completed the pedagogic phase with their work on 'Hard Days Night', also the soundtrack to a movie devised by United Artists solely as a scam for them to make money from the inevitable million selling soundtrack album (it sold 5 million).

Allegro *Goon* Troppo

The Beatles, George Martin and the director Richard Lester, all fans (or collaborators) of The Goons (a BBC radio show), collectively produced 'Hard Days Night'. A brilliant single, iconic movie which helped invent the MTV video format, and their first fully self-penned album. All captured by the memorably heutagogic Ringoism of the title.

So by their third album, The Beatles had perfected their pedagogic apprenticeship in the discipline of making hit records *for* the music business. However they had also transformed the expectations of the music listening public, recorded several classics beloved of fans and developed a sophisticated creative process working collaboratively as a group. Lennon and McCartney initially worked out new songs face-to-face in a style developed in Liverpool, fortified by tea, toast and 'ciggies'. They demonstrated songs in the studio to develop harmonies with Harrison, who also worked out a guitar solo while the classically trained George Martin worked out how best to record the songs in terms of musical arrangements and the sonic affordances of Abbey Road Studio

2. Finally Ringo, weakened by a childhood illness, listened intently before producing rhythms that served the song. The Beatles collaboratively produced perfectly recorded songs, the mark of their crafty pedagogic excellence.

You could not improve on 'Hard Days Night', it showed that The Beatles had learnt their lessons well, perfected them and in so doing changed the rules of the game. In the summer of 1964 they had provided the template for the 'self-contained rock band' which, while easing the path of those that followed, also offered a new challenge in terms of quality. Tim Riley says in 'Tell Me Why' (2006) that they had moved 'Beyond Adolescence' with the 'idea of an album as . . . a forum for ideas'.

The Social Context of The Beatles

Baudelaire (1821–67) said that nations get great men in spite of themselves and perhaps that was the case with The Beatles. Growing up in the fifties they were part of a generation in debt to their elders who had won the war but lost a peace measured out in rations. As Pete Townsend astutely pointed out, the 'restless generation' of the fifties was constantly reminded about the debt that they owed to their elders and moral superiors. The British 1944 Education Act raised the school-leaving age to 15, creating the possibility of secondary education for all, but without any real opportunities for taking advantage of it socially (Dunford and Sharp, 1990). Concerned with social justice the Beveridge Report (1942) sought to remove 'squalor, ignorance, want, idleness and disease', and a burgeoning class of educated working class kids began entering society in the fifties. The Robbins Report (1963) wouldn't open up Higher Education until the late sixties. Thus, The Beatles grew up in a social context designed to broaden their horizons educationally, while making them feel guilty and morally inferior. The single most significant act in The Beatles creating themselves as a group was McCartney turning down an apprenticeship to join the band full time, without knowing what that meant. That act of McCartney represents a shift from 'restless' fifties thinking to more of a 'reckless' sixties attitude.

The long-standing custom of making music in the home combined with the tradition of British music hall, still thriving in pre-television fifties and often the family choice of entertainment, meant that music making was strongly embedded socially in the fifties.

The Beatles themselves grew up in music-making families, McCartney's father was even a band leader, but the group also benefitted when hire purchase allowed for the long march to consumerism through radios and record players and then singles and albums. Beatlemania signified the arrival of a generation who were music-consuming fans, who wanted a spectacle previously consumed on TV, rather than music-making fans who loved listening to The Beatles as great live performers of music.

The Beatles became memorable because they didn't do what was expected, they didn't play what was expected and so sounded refreshingly different.

Phase 2: 1964–6

Andragogic excellence; from romantic to Romantic

Having proved themselves in the school of hit records, The Beatles grew in confidence between the return from their first visit to the United States and the end of their second visit in August 1964. Lennon published his book of 'nonsense' *In His Own Write* (1964) and was interviewed on highbrow BBC programmes. They were embarking on the andragogic phase of their learning.

This phase was mostly about the newly confident, professional Beatles relaxing and being able to reconnect with music, becoming the explorative fans that they really were, rather than pupils taking instruction from a master. They held court in clubs such as the Scotch of St James, where they mixed with their musical peers and social equals, the Stones, The Moody Blues, The Who and The Animals, as more groups broke through with new ideas, from Art Schools, Ealing, the Thames Delta and the provinces. This allowed The Beatles to share musical ideas with their contemporaries rather than borrow from their antecedents.

In 'Long and Winding Roads', Kenneth Womack (2007) sees the focus of The Beatles work as being 'musical creation' and in their andragogic phase this is what The Beatles turned to, first exploring paths suggested by others. These included Dylan, The Byrds, The Beach Boys, The Stones and The Who, synthesizing their influences into arguably the first rock album, 'Rubber Soul'.

Dylanesque; with friends . . .

The Beatles played Shea Stadium, New York, in 1964 to close their triumphant American tour and went to the legendary Delmonico's to celebrate. There they met Bob Dylan who dismissed their silly love songs and gave them a more Romantic vision of what they could do. George Harrison had played Dylan's second album relentlessly until both Lennon and McCartney became fans. Harrison also befriended Dave Crosby of The Byrds whose folk-rock sound would make them America's answer to The Beatles and ultimately influence 'Rubber Soul'. Folk-rock comes from a tradition that is more concerned with social protest than 'Moon-in-June' romance. The metacognitive inventiveness that they had already applied to their music began to be applied to their lyrics.

Their next album, the ironically entitled 'Beatles for Sale', featuring an exhausted looking foursome on the cover, opened with the Dylanesque 'Lennon Trilogy', including their scheduled next single 'I'm A Loser'. At the last minute, EMI demanded a happier tune and overnight, again, Lennon reeled off the cheerfully classic rocker 'I Feel Fine' that, coupled with 'She's A Woman', reflecting another Beatles trope of outstanding B-sides to great singles.

In the lands of the Fifth Beatles

So their andragogic phase, from June 1964 to April 1966 was one of listening, trying out new musical ideas, extending the limited range of Merseybeat, collaborating with others, examining ways of extending their skill as musicians, lyricists and songwriters as well as exploring the studio. While, at the same time of course, still fulfilling their obligations as the world's greatest group and living up to the ridiculous expectations of their fans. Somehow the witty and creative Beatles almost always had the British public on their side, largely because they were working class boys who had made good nationally. Previously being a middle manager in a minor company might have been the limit of their ambitions. Britain loved them because, for the first time since World War Two, the British could be seen as demonstrably better at something than was the rest of the world.

As well as Britain becoming a nation of supportive Fifth Beatles, the musical competition raised its game and 1965 saw a string of original hit records. Dylan, influenced in part by The Beatles, went electric and released the magisterial 'Like A Rolling Stone', The Rolling Stones went global with 'Satisfaction' and The Who burst through with the single that claimed the decade for youth; 'My Generation'. Arguably 1965 was the best year for 'pop' 'hit records' ever (Rolling Stone Magazine) and a Beatles single wasn't a shoo-in for years best. Their second film 'Help!' had, to some extent, sidelined them as creative pop musicians; it seemed they might be resting on their laurels as they became 'extras in their own movie'.

Bringing the future back home

Although George Martin recognized that he had become a collaborator on 'Yesterday', Help itself was a second consecutive 'incomplete' Beatles album. However great musical artists usually bounce back reflecting on learning from their failures. The Beatles response to being encouraged by their peers was 'Rubber Soul'. Arguably the finest album of the first half of the sixties offering a new template: the self-contained rock band *consciously* producing an album as cultural artefact. I remember thinking at the time that The Beatles were like scouts of popular culture exploring other artists on our behalf, bringing back what they had learnt and presenting a fresh synthesis enabling us to benefit from their experiments. In Open Context Model terms, they listened to the heutagogues, remixed it and offered a new orthodoxy. They synthesized the future, presenting it afresh so others could learn.

'Rubber Soul' was a great rock album where The Beatles synthesized Dylan, The Byrds, themselves (Lennon on ballads, McCartney on rockers), The Kinks, The Who, The Animals, The Moody Blues, new instruments (electric pianos, acoustic guitars) and new studio affordances. 'Rubber Soul' presented The Beatles as a rock band who had learnt from their friends and were playing songs for their peers.

Phase 3: 1966–7

Heutagogic excellence; from hit album to cultural artefact

Bookending The Beatles heutagogic period were twin attacks on print formats. In 'Paperback Writer' McCartney boasted that if you liked the style he 'could turn it round' and in 'I Am The Walrus', Lennon delivered a nonsense poem about nonsense poems, containing probably his most visceral attack on the British Establishment. Heutagogy is about playing with form and The Beatles did this explicitly and implicitly within their heutagogic period, which lasted from 13 April 1966 ('Paperback Writer') to 27 August 1967 (the death of their manager Brian Epstein).

If we use metaphors to characterize The Beatles' 'learning' periods then the pedagogic phase was their formal time in the classroom of George Martin. The andragogic phase was their time in the playground learning informally from their friends and the heutagogic phase was their time in the workshop of Abbey Road Studio 2. They became skilled craftsmen inventing new musical processes and this hands-on time in the studio is why I separate 'Rubber Soul' from 'Revolver', unlike George Harrison who sees them as a creative pair, as they shift from andragogy to heutagogy. 'Revolver', which took three times longer to record, developed when they started playing in the studio and building unique soundscapes for each song. This created a qualitative difference from 'Rubber Soul', where the folk-rock inspired sounds remain essentially the same throughout, with some colourful additions like the sitar in 'Norwegian Wood'. Moreover, 'Revolver' sustains this invention and includes a new collaborator, 20-year-old Geoff Emerick. 'Golden Ears' as he was called, joined them as a studio engineer on 'Revolver' extending their sonic range.

The golden sounds of 'Revolver'

The Beatles always refused to repeat themselves and it is 'Revolver's' sonics that allows it to shine on brightly down the years. On Harrison's 'Taxman', the whump of the bass comes from using a loudspeaker as a microphone, 'Eleanor Rigby' features a double string quartet, 'I'm Only Sleeping' has backwards guitars and sitar like sounds while, just four tracks in, there is a real sitar track 'Love You Too' recorded collaboratively with Indian musicians in London. 'Here, There and Everywhere', Emerick's favourite track, features Alan Civil's French horn before everyone has fun simulating life underwater on 'Yellow Submarine'. Side one of 'Revolver' was their most sustained and inventive side of music, yet side two matches it for creativity before climaxing with the endless two minutes of 'Tomorrow Never Knows'. The Beatles had created an album that was completely inventive from beginning to end; even the album sleeve was by artistic collaborator Klaus Voorman, an old friend since Hamburg. 'Revolver' is so distinctive musically that online music magazine Pitchfork refuses to discuss the greatest album of the 1960s as 'Revolver's ego is out of hand'.

Although 'Rubber Soul's' sonics are relatively limited by its folk-rock concern it was a big step forward lyrically. 'Revolver's' sounds are particularly polished but lyrically it also builds on their emerging romantic vision. 'Revolver' was very English, in Bracewell's sense of being concerned with a 'dreamy Albion', yet with a wholly unusual worldview located somewhere in the twentieth century.

Heutagogy in the Studio

Tomas Eerola (1996) of the Dutch media research group 'soundscapes' defines this peak productive period as their 'experimental style', measured in terms of the differences from the original Mersey Beat. The song-based experimentations that made 'Revolver' so distinctive were synthesized and became the basis of their heutagogic phase. Eerola usefully identifies the *most* creative period of The Beatles recording life as being very precisely from 'Strawberry Fields Forever' to 'I Am The Walrus'. Interestingly, the 'Magical Mystery Tour' album, a release oddity, has sold enduringly well containing the tracks 'Penny Lane' and 'Strawberry Fields Forever' making it equally as representative of their creative and 'experimental style' as Sgt Pepper's Lonely Hears Club Band. Both albums contain five of The Beatles' most creative tracks. Eerola (1996) notes that many of The Beatles most popular songs are among their most 'experimental': meaning that this heutagogic creativity was also deeply satisfying to the listening public.

Creative nostalgia

Tim Riley (2001) suggests that the subject of The Beatles work is 'nostalgia' and while 'Strawberry Fields Forever' is also about 'musical creation'; from the opening Mellotron flutes to its backwards ending. Ironically, this nostalgic reflection on their origins, initiated with 'In My Life' on 'Rubber Soul', was matched by their greatest phase of musical experimentation and enabled their greatest re-invention.

'Sgt Peppers' itself was a creative metaphor that allowed The Beatles to transform themselves into recording artists once they became the first band to retire from playing live in 1966. Ironically the album from which their original 'scouse' character was most absent provided their greatest success with the cultural elite in London. On 'Sgt Peppers' they were curating someone else's album, 'The Lonely Hearts Club Band', which enabled them to extend their creative palette and their ability to play with form musically. 'Sgt Peppers' as an album is an enduring cultural artefact and was also as a massive media event representing the high water mark of the 'Summer of Love' in 1967.

After Sergeant Pepper

While 'Sgt Peppers' was their longest period of just playing the studio, they continued playing with form thereafter, representing Britain on the first global TV programme 'Our World', with 'All You Need is Love', before starting to prepare the self-directed film 'Magical Mystery Tour'. They also linked up with the Mahesh Maharishi Yogi to take up meditation. The pace of their experimentation seemed to be speeding up. Then Brian Epstein died. From 27 August 1967 onwards The

Beatles would have to make their own business decisions and just as Lennon was singing, 'I am he as you are me as we are altogether', they weren't anymore. With Epstein's death the support network of collaborators and the contexts from which they grew their most creatively successful processes was rent asunder. Their learning was over and everything was about to change.

The Open Context Model of The Beatles

Originally a friend asked if I could use The Beatles to exemplify the Open Context Model but I was sceptical. However once I had defined the parameters, pedagogy as hit records, andragogy as peer collaboration, heutagogy as playing with the studio, it quickly made sense, providing fresh insights into The Beatles and how they made music; while also providing insight into the value of other commentators on their work. This approach allows for a very precise yet somewhat different chunking up of their career. Eerola, and others, argue that 'Yesterday' is the switch from their earlier career into their 'mature phase'. The PAH Continuum allows for a different analysis of the phases of their career starting with drafting in Ringo Starr on drums on 28 August 1962 and ending with the death of Brian Epstein on 28 August 1967.

My concern in this context has been with how they learnt about recording hit records rather than with their career overall. From this perspective we can see that originally The Beatles looked up to established artists and covered their songs while writing lyrically rather simplistic songs themselves. Once they had a recording contract with George Martin he helped them with their song-writing but, more crucially, with how you turn songs into hit records. He re-arranged the musical elements that The Beatles brought him and together they created the Mersey Beat, which dominated and transformed the British music scene for the next 18 months. This allowed both copyists, such as The Fourmost, and other young musicians with different sensibilities and influences, such as blues aficionados the Rolling Stones, to emerge. Two years into their recording career, The Beatles had their peers to talk to and learn from rather than older American musicians. Notably in London they befriended other provincial artists, The Animals from Newcastle and the Moody Blues from Birmingham, signifying the peer influences of their andragogic phase. By definition their heutagogic phase could be described as peerless. They uniquely gave up touring in August 1966, but had already begun to make the studio into another instrument on 'Revolver'. The Beatles were such good musicians that Walter Everett devotes a two-volume book *The Beatles as Musicians* (1999) to their qualities. George

Martin said that initially he played arrangements to them on the piano which they didn't understand, however within a year they had mastered it for themselves. 'Strawberry Fields Forever' was written while Lennon was making a film but the music was begun by McCartney playing the Mellotron he found on Lennon's staircase.

The Beatles re-configured themselves as a metaphor, 'Sgt Pepper', to free themselves up to experiment. Eerola's analysis of their 'experimental' style shows that they peaked in terms of this musical style during 1967, but this is a musicologist analysis and ignores how they used the studio and the value of Martin's 'inventive arrangements and playful effects' (Riley, 2011).

So we can see that the high water mark of The Beatles' creativity as defined by Eerola, was also their heutagogic phase, of playing with form. The Open Context Model of Learning informs us that to get to this peak they needed to master the pedagogic phase, with George Martin, and deepen their collaborations and influences in the andragogic phase by finding peers they could work and share their ideas with in order to create the support network from which their heutagogic creativity could finally emerge.

References

Beveridge, W. (1942), *Report of the Inter-Departmental Committee on Social Insurance and Allied Services.* London: His Majesty's Stationary Office.

Bracewell, M. (2009), *England Is Mine; Pop Life in Albion.* London: Faber.

Committee on Higher Education (23 September 1963), *Higher Education: Report of the Committee Appointed by the Prime Minister under the Chairmanship of Lord Robbins 1961–63*, Cmnd. 2154, London: HMSO.

Dunford, J. and Sharp, P. (1990), *The Education System in England and Wales.* Essex: Longman.

Eerola, T. (1996), *The Rise and Fall of the Experimental Style of the Beatles*, Groningen. Retrieved 31 May 2012 from: www.icce.rug.nl/~soundscapes/VOLUME03/Rise_and_fall0.shtml.

Emerick, G. (2007), *Here, There and Everywhere.* London: Gotham Books.

Everett, W. (1999), *The Beatles as Musicians.* Oxford: Oxford University Press.

Frame, P. (2007), *The Restless Generation.* London: Rogan House.

Gladwell, M. (2008), *Outliers: The Story of Success.* London: Allen Lane.

Gruber, H. (1989), *The Evolving Systems Approach to Creative Work.* In D. Wallace and H. Gruber (eds), *Creative People at Work.* New York: Oxford University Press, 23.

Lewisohn, M. (2010), *The Beatles Chronicles.* Chicago: Chicago Review Press.

Luckin, R., Clark, W., Garnett, F. et al. (2010), 'Learner Generated Contexts: a framework to support the effective use of technology to support learning', in M. J. W. Lee and C. McLoughlin (eds), *Web 2.0-Based E-Learning: Applying Social Informatics for Tertiary Teaching*. Hershey, PA: IGI Global, 35.

Lennon, J. (1964), *In His Own Right*. London: John Lennon.

Martin, G. (1994), *All You Need Is Ears*. London: St Martins Press.

Miles, B. (1998), *Many Years from Now*. London: Holt.

Pitchfork. Retrieved 31 May 2012 from: http://pitchfork.com/features/staff-lists/6405-the-200-greatest-songs-of-the-1960s/.

Riley, T. (2002), *Tell Me Why*. Cambridge: Da Capo.

—. (2011), *Lennon*. London: Virgin Books.

Rolling Stone. Retrieved 31 May 2012 from: www.rollingstone.com/news/coverstory/500songs.

Womack, K. (2007), *Long and Winding Roads*. London: Continuum.

9

Putting Heutagogy into Learning

Fred Garnett and Ronan O'Beirne

Summary

In this chapter we outline how a group of researchers, teachers, librarians and policy-makers, working in technology-enabled community settings, developed a range of new learning technologies and resources. While those technologies in themselves are not important here, our reflection identifies that they played an important part in defining an approach to learning that significantly departed from traditional pedagogies typically seen in similar community settings. Our discussion outlines a sequence of interpretations of andragogical and then heutagogical characteristics that can be associated with those learning instances. Our ideas developed in three phases which gives a natural structure to the journey: Community Learning and Andragogy; Making Content 'Fit for Context'; and Open Learning and Heutagogy.

Community learning and andragogy

The authors have both worked with information technology in community learning settings since the late 1990s. We have had experience in designing learning using web and internet technologies, running community centres and being responsive to the learning needs of the socially excluded.

The basis of our findings is grounded in practical work with these communities of learners. Our participant observation approach to understanding the deeper motivations and outcomes of learning can be seen both as our methodology and as a (necessary) precursor to our theorizing (Bourdieu, 1977). We undertook practical engagement with a number of community projects and, through reflective practice, we then began to theorize.

Looking at the wider context it is of interest perhaps to note that the main driver for the funding of community networking at the time was not exclusively education focused. It was essentially a socio-economic policy that was delivered in the new millennium in the United Kingdom under a new government led by Tony Blair. During the period 1998 to 2005 there was an upsurge in community networking with initiatives such as Brixton On-line and Shipley Communities On-line, serving as examples of grassroots implementations of national policies on social inclusion, digital citizenship and lifelong learning. The presumption by the policy-makers was that by putting technology into community centres social impact would follow. From an urban regeneration perspective there would be an increase in skills and in turn, lower levels of unemployment localized within those communities. The evidence from a number of projects suggests that indeed this was the case. However, what we witnessed was a more profound impact on peoples' lives in terms of their learning. This 'disconnect' between policy objectives and actual effects, according to Malin and Knapp (1997, p. 419) defies, 'explanation in part because the social conditions to be attended are tangled webs of problems with symptoms, sources, and "solutions" that are neither readily apparent nor reliably addressed by policy provisions'. We would agree this is the case but would extend this to suggest that technology now plays a significant part in the complex mix of symptoms, sources and solutions.

As our work became included in national initiatives as part of the £250m Community Action for Lifelong Learning programme (Education for Change, 2006), we realized that existing subject-driven pedagogies were not capturing what we were discovering about how people learnt in community settings with new technologies, especially the web. We identified as one of the most significant characteristics the break in the hierarchical relation between teacher, learning resource and learner. In the traditional model the teacher provided the learning resource or content, on which the learning was based and with which the learner was required to engage. In the model we were observing learners, now enabled by technology, were able to acquire learning resources of their own volition. In other words, they could simply go online and gain access to material that they found relevant and useful. This sense that technology was shifting the locus of control from teacher to learner was of significance within a community setting where learning resources in the physical sense (books and audio-visual materials, for example) had always been scarce. Moreover, the changing power relation in terms of the control of knowledge in a community setting was important. The authors recognized the potential benefit of increased engagement to learners in a situation where their own learning content was the basis of their learning. This was particularly evident in the creation of new content by learners themselves.

Elsewhere in the wider learning environment, particularly formal education, there was significant growth in computer-assisted learning and debates about e-learning pedagogies became prominent (Laurillard, 1993; Salmon, 2000). Mostly these debates were focused on technology and its novel uses while assuming that the pedagogy of the teacher's authority and power, and crucially, their control of knowledge, would be sustained. One critical point here is the power relation that is vested in the learning resource. This is an interesting issue and can usefully be related to Foucault and Gordon's (1980) knowledge and power theory. It is an area that is under-researched in terms of andragogy and heutagogy but one we see as important in informal and formal learning: for example the virtual learning environment and Foucault's panopticon.

As the potential benefits of a networked society became apparent policy-makers, particularly those in education, sought to exploit the opportunity. Following the election of Tony Blair and New Labour in 1997 the holy grail of delivering education via 'e-learning' became a policy imperative and a number of initiatives, starting with *learndirect*, the 'University for Industry' and the National Grid for Learning for schools, were funded. It was quickly established, however, that creating electronic learning materials through which the learner would navigate in a linear fashion was not only expensive to produce but the structure and content was not engaging. It should be noted that there was also impressive competition emerging from the games industry. There was a growing excitement then, within formal learning circles, that the notion of sharing digital learning objects was seen as a remedy to the high cost and poor quality of e-learning. The National Learning Network policy initiative, for example, was funded to put Virtual Learning Environments into every Further Education College in order to use expensively commissioned learning objects.

At the 1999 invitational DCMI (Dublin Core Metadata Initiative) workshop held in Frankfurt, attended by one of the authors, the Dublin Core Education Community was formed. Its aim was to enable sharing and interoperability of learning objects. The implications of metadata use on the wider web community was profound and in fact can be seen to have provided much of the underlying architecture to many of today's systems. It was quickly understood in educational circles, and particularly in educational publishing, that the ability to share learning content would be a significant 'game changer'. Once learning objects in digital format had been assigned metadata using one of the emerging standards such as SCORM (Sharable Content Object Reference Model) those objects could be reused and deployed in a range of learning settings. Perhaps of even more significance, creating learning objects of whatever size or format, so long as they were digital, was now a straightforward task that could be carried out by anyone. Moreover, good metadata allowed learning objects to be stored and retrieved effectively. It was presumed that digital content in community networks, created by learners and 'painted up' with its metadata would be shareable and re-useable.

We extended our research to consider how learners might share resources and how this might create a second wider online community. With funding secured through a government agency our MCC (Metadata for Community Content) project sought to explore how informal learning resources, once they had been assigned metadata, could be shared across a network of UK Online centres. UK Online centres were typically sited within community venues such as youth centres, public libraries and community and village halls: their overarching remit being to provide access to technology. As a part of the MCC project we investigated how people were learning in these new contexts, what pedagogies might best describe this learning process and how we might design better learning processes to support this, others (Smith and Cook, 2002) evaluated the wider aspects of the MCC project.

The MCC project sought to enable the sharing of electronic learning resources by encouraging learners to assign metadata to the learning objects which they themselves had created. Unfortunately as we noted in retrospect the whole enterprise was based on an assumption of a model of scarcity; in other words that learning content was scarce and its retrieval difficult unless highly structured metadata was in place. An analogy can be drawn here with the library where one needs accurate information (metadata) to retrieve the relevant book. What we were beginning to witness in our observations was that this so-called scarcity model of resources was rapidly giving way to an abundance model. It was predicated by the ability of learners to copy digital content without any intellectual property rights restrictions and, at the press of a button transmit that knowledge across the globe. Quite simply and suddenly the learner was empowered.

The MCC project can now be seen largely as insignificant because the challenge of assigning metadata outweighed the usefulness of doing so. Metadata, in as much as it could be understood by those outside the technical field, seemed to have little point for the individual learner. Indeed, Currier et al. (2004) note difficulties with this approach across a range of settings including community learning.

Another factor that may have played a part was the position of the learners within this wider resource-sharing online community. In essence, the learners were interested in their own communities and did not consider themselves to be part of a wider learning community, hence their reluctance to become involved. On reflection, we debated whether this could be considered to be one of the drawbacks of andragogy and heutagogy, where a sense of the individual rather than the cooperative or collaborative nature is likely to be in the ascendancy. Through our exploration of metadata we gained an insight into the learners' perceptions of their learning objects or resources. This also pointed to some more complex issues around 'knowledge' and 'authority' and to the willingness of these learners to create and manage their own resources. Our presumption at the outset of the MCC project was that, from a pedagogical perspective, there needed to be some authority that controlled learning resources upon which the learning was based. Our findings at the end provided an insight into how knowledge and its control are central to a learning environment. This helped us to develop our understanding of andragogy and heutagogy.

We differentiate here between learning to use the technologies and using the technologies to learn: the former being a prerequisite to the latter. Certainly the former occurred and by and large was a process grounded in a didactic model. However, the real focus of our work is on the latter. That is, how those learners within the community, once they had been equipped with the hardware and know-how, extended their horizons and undertook self-directed learning.

The dominant frameworks of digital literacy that emerged suggested that as a precursor to learn in a digital world a level of e-literacy, although not clearly defined, needed to be achieved (O'Beirne, 2005). Learners appeared to be engaged initially on a basis of basic need but as they became more skilled and knowledgeable with the technology, they became interested in publishing their own material. This may be seen now as a natural path for learners to follow. At the time, this was in contrast to the existing highly structured formal learning progression route, which had a number of assessment points that impeded the learners' progress. In a sense the andragogic learner can be seen to be rejecting the constraints of a disempowering pedagogy. The first phase of this that we witnessed was learners taking control of their content. But this was not enough. Learners also need to control the context of their learning; if content was king then to be sure context was queen.

Making content 'fit for context'

The second phase of our incorporation of heutagogy into our learning modelling came out of a commission to create socially inclusive learning content for UK online centres. As a part of the development process we held an online conference with the Content Bank group in the United States, a part of the Digital Divide Network, who had been involved in researching content for CTCnet community technology centres. Commissioned by President Clinton these technology centres had very similar characteristics to UK Online centres. Content Bank itself had emerged from research by the Children's Partnership (Lazarus and Mora) into what constituted socially inclusive online content for 'under-served Americans', as they described it, and had identified two key factors. First, they found that access to the internet, a key policy objective of community technology centres in both the United States and the United Kingdom at the time, while critical, wasn't in itself socially inclusive. Secondly, they found that existing online content reinforced social exclusion, as it was written by and for a narrowly defined audience: this was pre-Web2.0. The researchers then supplied guidelines of what constituted relevant content and Content Bank had been commissioned to address this.

Our week-long online conference on 'digital divide content' also involved many UK practitioners from the DfES Cybrarian project and NOF Community Grids for Learning programme. Sharing our divergent practice and experiences enabled us to conclude that we needed to develop content-creation toolkits as socially inclusive learning content needs to be both specific and contextualized. We saw this contextual content creation process existing in a web of relationships between learners, trusted intermediaries, such as peers and mentors, learning support workers and the professional 'infomediaries' who maintained Community Grids for Learning. It was a form of systemic co-creation, with fairly clear if distributed roles. It was from what we had learnt through the online conference that we coined the phrase 'context is queen'. Because of the identified need to contextualize learning resources in original ways, in part to enable what we had also identified as 'community-responsive curricula' (another way of describing the contextualizing process we had identified), we realized that we needed to add a further dimension to our work on modelling informal learning. One author suggested that we needed to investigate ideas in heutagogy. However, we initially saw incorporating heutagogy into informal e-learning as an aspiration to help us make sense of the process of contextualizing learning. We didn't at that time see heutagogy as being an element of a new, more open and collaborative pedagogy, which reflected the affordances of emerging Web 2.0 tools like social networks. We were still reflecting more on how we might develop our modelling of informal e-learning in community settings.

One practical consequence of the Digital Divide Content Debate was the design of the Adult and Community Learning Network (www.aclearn.net), an LSE-funded national adult and community learning resource. This contained a section with content-creation toolkits, for example a hosted WebQuest toolkit, with which community learning practitioners could create content locally. In an interview with the developer of WebQuests at San Diego State University we learned that WebQuests treat 'surfing as learning' reflecting the increasing agency allowed to learners online.

Learner-Generated Contexts Research Group (LGC)

Following the end of the MCC project the authors became involved in a new informal research group formed in late 2006. This group comprised a range of people who had collaborated on developing a social network-learning tool, as part of the government-funded Cybrarian project, along with other researchers. The LGC was a self-organized interdisciplinary, cross-sectoral research group concerned to identify the nature of learning in a post-Web 2.0 world, where User Generated Content was becoming ubiquitous. At their initial workshop they identified that as learner-generated content became common then making that content 'fit for context' would become the next critical issue in learning and what was needed was an understanding of 'learner-generated contexts'. This is perhaps currently reflected in the ongoing debates about Open Learning and the role of universities. LGC was an informal unfunded research group that became based at the London

Knowledge Laboratory. However, members had a range of backgrounds covering universities, colleges, community, libraries and informatics and this range helped shape the third phase of our thinking.

Open learning and heutagogy

The UK Open University launched its Open Learn initiative in November 2007 with a conference on open learning. This had a focus on making traditional university learning resources available outside of institutions. As a group, LGC decided that it should apply what we had learnt about creating informal e-learning processes to a new, broader 'pedagogy' needed to make open learning work across a range of learning contexts. This also became our opportunity to examine how we might incorporate heutagogy practically into our theoretical approaches to modelling informal learning. As our group included researchers and practitioners from all sectors of learning in the United Kingdom we could broaden our theory out from its community learning-based origins to become a 'multi-contexts' theory.

Luckin's Ecology of Resources Model (Luckin, 2010) concerning how resources were used for learning also provided us with a multi-context framework on which to base our discussions. Part of the actual process of developing what became the Open Context Model of Learning was carried out collaboratively online, using a wiki, as it involved several authors from across the United Kingdom. The Open Context Model of Learning came from the confluence of these two framing concepts, the ecology of resources and the model of informal e-learning. The cross-sectoral expertise of the group enabled us to develop a multi-context model of learning for a post-Web 2.0 world. Within this model we incorporated heutagogy into a new pedagogy-andragogy-heutagogy (PAH) Continuum. In the PAH Continuum we look at how the pedagogic practice of subject delivery, in its many variants, might be broadened by the more collaborative strategies that our informal e-learning work had revealed. As the understanding we had gained in using andragogic concepts to enable us to develop a model of informal e-learning, shifted to thoughts of using heutagogic concepts to help us reflect about open learning in a post-Web 2.0 world, we drew two key conclusions.

First that LGC should articulate its learning models without reference to specific technologies, or even technology at all. In the PAH Continuum, described more fully below, we show this by creating a range of metaphors for each approach to learning. We did this because the PAH Continuum isn't a literal continuum; it is more of a development framework for thinking about learning and teaching strategies and relationships.

Secondly we realized that our practice and reflection had led us to a position about the future of e-learning which suggested that e-learning represented more of a superset of learning possibilities, whereas it is more typically treated as a subset. For example, UK institutional and policy formulations as articulated by the Higher Education Funding Council sees e-learning as being a subset of the distance learning offer, which is itself a subset of the overall learning offer of a University.

The PAH Continuum

The Open Context Model of Learning has been fully documented in a recent book chapter (Luckin et al., 2010), but the key element within it is the PAH Continuum. Table 9.1 represents how we collaboratively evolved our thinking about modelling informal e-learning to create a multi-context pedagogy designed to anticipate the era of open learning. The PAH Continuum represents a mixed use of: pedagogy (understanding the subject matter of learning activities in a way that enables the production of learning resources by the teacher); andragogy (supporting the collaborative processes of the learning group, including negotiating the content and sequencing of learning such that communications around shared work amplifies participant understanding of the subject and can lead to group work for formative assessment); and heutagogy (enabling the development of original responses to the learning being engaged in by learners, including co-creation, and original ways of presenting work for summative assessment).

The purpose of the PAH Continuum was to take what we had learnt about the value of learner modelling, and about modelling learning using our practice and our reflections upon informal e-learning, in order to help how we might think about learning in post-Web 2.0 contexts. It represents an early, if informed,

Table 9.1 The PAH Continuum

	Pedagogy	**Andragogy**	**Heutagogy**
Locus of control	Teacher	Teacher/learner	Learner
Education sector	School	Adult	Research
Cognition level	Cognition	Meta-cognition	Epistemic cognition
Knowledge production context	Subject understanding	Process negotiation	Context shaping

formulation of such ideas. We see the PAH Continuum as a framework to help develop new thinking about learning as the fault lines between education as a system and learning as a process are deepened by the collaborative affordances of social networks and new technology. We present it as a continuum – but continua are dangerous in education. They can be interpreted as being progress points along the learning journey so that one presumes, wrongly, that the learner moves simply from pedagogy to heutagogy. However, any value in incorporating heutagogy, what Hase and Kenyon (Chapter 2) call 'self-determined learning' into learner-modelling for an open learning era might best be discerned in practical applications

Practical applications of our theoretical framework (PAH Continuum)

A theoretical framework for learner-modelling has many advantages, but is most useful if it helps the learning process in any context. Chapter 8 of this book provides an example of how the PAH Continuum can be used retrospectively to analyse creative processes. Nonetheless, our interest here is in designing learning in a range of contexts that allow for multiple navigation strategies through the learning process, which are largely determined by the learner. Fortunately we have the practical example of Dr Thomas Cochrane at Unitec in Auckland, New Zealand, who found our work on the web and applied the PAH Continuum to the design of the four-year BA in Product Design. His concern was with how mobile technologies could be used by learners as they increasingly took control over their learning over a four-year design course. Significantly the Product Design degree isn't built around a structured syllabus with a focus on content but rather is based on practical work and increasing self-determination. This craft-based degree, where students are aiming to produce their own work to professional standards, uses a framework based on the PAH Continuum, designed to enable learner self-direction while staff focus on supporting learning (Cochrane, 2010).

We have used the PAH Continuum to analyse the role of teachers (Ecclesfield and Garnett, 2013), as part of the University of Glamorgan 'Working Lives' project, and as part of the LSIS research project on 'Digital Practitioners' (Rebbeck et al., 2012).

We also incorporated the PAH Continuum into the Emergent Learning Model (Garnett and Ecclesfield, 2009) from which two projects have been developed. First the Ambient Learning City project, Mosi-Along, where the social media participation model of Aggregate then Curate (Whitworth et al., 2012) was developed to reflect the agency of learners as they moved between online and real worlds. Secondly the WikiQuals project, where the self-determination of learners in a post-hoc accreditation process is being examined through an 'affinity-based' approach. These new learning models, and the attendant projects, are still in the early stages of being tested and it is too early to know if they may have lasting value. However, their development is based on new ways of structuring heutagogy to help design new learning processes and the early findings begin to suggest that heutagogy is a key concept in designing learning in a Web 2.0 world.

Conclusion

We theorized, in sociological terms, how Bourdieu's (1977) concept of agency and structure can be related to community e-learning. The 'field' of Bourdieu can in a sense be considered to be the space in which competition over resources takes place. Our understanding of both andragogy and heutagogy can be enhanced when they are considered in the wider context of Bourdieu's concepts of field, habitus and capital (Grenfell, 2008). Our contribution to knowledge is: to provide a pragmatic understanding of andragogy and heutagogy; to place the PAH Continuum in a wider context; and to associate and extend the theories of Pierre Bourdieu to the virtual world of learning.

In broader terms, heutagogy can be seen as a key component in responding to Web 2.0 affordances and understanding new modes of learning in the changing public context of our transition from social hierarchies to social networks: as Ben Hammersley put it in the British Council Lecture of 2011, 'An Internet of People'. We need to design new approaches to learning, and to create new contexts for learning that reflect an emerging networked digital society rather than a mechanical, industrial one. We commend heutagogic learning, and thinking, as the missing link in this process.

References

Bourdieu, P. (1977), *Outline of a Theory of Practice*. Cambridge, UK: Cambridge University Press.

Cochrane, T. (2010), 'Exploring mobile learning success factors', *ALT-J, Research in Learning Technology*, 18(2), 133–48.

Currier, S., Barton, J., O'Beirne, R. and Ryan, B. (2004), 'Quality assurance for digital learning object repositories: issues for the metadata creation process', *Association for Learning Technology Journal*, 12(1), 5–20.

Digital Divide Network (archive). Retrieved 31 May 2012 from: www.digitaldivide.net/.

Ecclesfield, N. and Garnett, F. (2013), 'New learners, new pedagogy: an emerging craft professionalism?', in L. Gornal, C. Cook, L. Daunton, J. Salisbury and B. Thomas (eds), *Academic Working Lives: Experience, Practice and Change.* London: Continuum, in press.

Education for Change (2006), *The Funds ICT Content Programme.* London: Big Lottery Fund.

Foucault, M. and Gordon, C. (1980), *Power/Knowledge: Selected Interviews and Other Writings, 1972–1977.* New York: Pantheon Books.

Garnett, F. and Ecclesfield, N. (2009), 'Proposed model of the relationships between informal, non-formal and formal learning'. Paper presented at the *IADIS International Conference on Cognition and Exploratory Learning in Digital Age (CELDA)*, Rome, Italy.

Grenfell, M. (2008), *Pierre Bourdieu: Key Concepts.* Stocksfield, England: Acumen.

Hammersley, B. (2011), *Annual Lecture 2011; An Internet of People.* British Council. Retrieved 31 May 2012 from: http://blog.britishcouncil.org/2011/03/annual-lecture-2011/.

Hase, S. and Kenyon, C. (2000), 'From andragogy to heutagogy', *Ultibase,* Royal Melbourne Institute of Technology, Melbourne.

Laurillard, D. (1993), Rethinking University Teaching: A Framework for the Effective Use of Educational Technology. London: Routledge.

Lazarus, W. and Mora, F. (2000), Online Content for Low-income and Underserved Americans: The Digital Divide's New Frontier. Santa Monica: Children's Partnership.

Luckin, R. (2010), *Redesigning Learning Contexts.* London: Routledge

Luckin, R., Clark, W., Garnett, F., Whitworth, A., Akass, J., Cook, J., Day, P., Ecclesfield, N., Hamilton, T. and Robertson, J. (2010), 'Learner generated contexts: a framework to support the effective use of technology to support learning', in M. J. W. Lee and C. McLoughlin (eds.) *Web 2.0-based e-learning: Applying Social Informatics for Tertiary Teaching.* Hershey, PA: IGI Global, 70–84.

Malin, B. and Knapp, M. (1997), 'Rethinking the multiple perspectives approach to education policy analysis: implications for policy practice connections'. *Journal of Education Policy*, 12(5), 419–45.

National Learning Network. Retrieved 31 May 2012 from: www.nln.ac.uk/.

O'Beirne, R. (2005), 'E-literacy and andragogy – a view through the Community Content Lens', *Journal of eLiteracy*, 2, 104–13.

Rebbeck, G., Ecclesfield, N. and Garnett, F. (2011), *The Digital Practitioner*, slides from an LSIS presentation. Retrieved 31 May 2012 from: www.slideshare.net/fredgarnett/digital-practitioner-2011.

Salmon, G. (2000), E-moderating: The Key to Teaching and Learning Online. London: Kogan Page.

Smith, M. and Cook, J. (2002), *Final Report for 'Study of UK Online Centres'*, Learning Technology Research Institute, London Metropolitan University. Retrieved 21 May 2012 from: www.londonmet.ac.uk/ltri/research/projects/ukonline.htm.

Whitworth, D., Garnett, F. and Pearson, D. (2012), 'Aggregate, then curate: digital learning champions and informational resources'. Paper presented at *Networked Learning Conference*, Maastricht, Holland.

WikiQuals. Retrieved 31 May 2012 from: http://wikiquals.wordpress.com/about/.

10

Lifelong Learning

Jane H. Eberle

Summary

Heutagogy with its feature of double-loop learning is not just for adult learners. In a global society in which the emphasis must be on problem solving, and critical and creative thinking, the practice of heutagogical tenets clearly focuses on ways in which to achieve these. This chapter will offer practical applications for all levels of learning and demonstrate ways to include even the most reluctant learners across their lifespan.

Double-loop learning

Heutagogy, or self-determined learning, encourages students to become active participants in what they are learning. Rather than using a single-loop model of learning in which the learner identifies a problem, takes action, produces an outcome and then begins again with a new problem, double-loop learning encourages students to reflect on their learning and to assess how it has changed their beliefs and actions and how they can apply what they have learned to other areas. Teachers become facilitators, not as leaders who sit back and let the students 'discover' their learning but as leaders who provide appropriate guidance, resources and models. While heutagogy may be considered an outgrowth from andragogy, a term coined by Malcolm Knowles (1984) that suggests self-directed learning in adult education, heutagogy (and andragogy) can be effectively used for elementary, secondary and adult learners.

Heutagogy envelops double-loop learning, which is defined by Argyris (n.d.) as:

> A higher order of learning is when the individual questions the goal structures and rules upon detecting an error. This is more like 'coloring outside the lines' to solve the problem or error. This is referred to as 'double-loop learning.' This is more creative and may lead to alterations in the rules, plans, strategies, or consequences initially related to the problem at hand. Double-loop learning involves critical reflection upon goals, beliefs, values, conceptual frameworks, and strategies.

> Argyris (n.d.) believes that this way of learning is critical in organizations and individuals that find themselves in rapidly changing and uncertain contexts (Figure 10.1).

Clark and Mayer (2011, p. 25) state that the challenge in any, 'learning program is to build lessons in ways that are compatible with human learning processes. To be effective, instructional strategies must support these processes. That is, they must foster the psychological events necessary for learning'.

Clark and Mayer define psychological engagement and the events that occur as a result in contrast to behavioural engagement and its events. These are addressed in Table 10.1.

While behavioural engagement has its place in a heutagogical environment, the psychological engagement with its constructivist type activities aligns with the tenets of heutagogical theory. Hase and Kenyon (2001) first defined heutagogy as, 'the study of self-determined learning' (p. 1), there have been some who argue that heutagogy is not a viable option for most higher learning. This chapter will argue that the reverse is true. Eberle and Childress (2006, p. 23) point out that,

> In a heutagogical approach to learning, the teacher serves as the facilitator allowing students to inquire, research, discover, analyze, and evaluate according

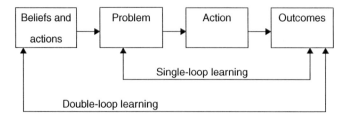

Figure 10.1 The flow of double-loop learning (from Eberlee and Childress, 2006).

Table 10.1 Clark and Mayer's (2011, p. 17) definitions of behavioural and psychological engagement

Type of engagement	Definition of engagement	E-learning activities associated with engagement
Behavioural	Any action a learner takes during an instructional episode	*Pressing forward arrow
		*Typing answer in response box
		*Clicking on an option from a multiple-choice menu
		*Verbally responding to an instructor's question
		*Self-explaining a complex visual
Psychological	Cognitive processing of content in ways that lead to acquisition of new knowledge and skills	*Summarizing a portion of the lesson
		*Generating an outline or drawing based on the lesson
		*Taking a practice test

to their needs and what is being studied. This is not a lesser role for the teacher but, rather, a different role from that of the pedagogist. The emphasis shifts from giver of knowledge to one who supports, encourages, challenges, questions, and promotes intellectual curiosity with the learner being held responsible for what is accomplished. Student-directed discussions that allow freedom of expression and thoughtful reflection promote clarity of ideas. Healthy debate is encouraged as a means to discovery of opposing views. Students are helped to narrow their interests in a topic, to reflect on what they have learned, and produce sound projects, papers, or whatever culminating activity is assigned or agreed upon. Along the way or after the fact, they may branch into other areas as a means to further challenge their own ideas and values. The sharing of activities increases the collaborative inquiry among students so that they may expand on what they learn from others, as well.

Stepping away from the pedagogical instructor role in a teacher-centred environment may be difficult for some. Learning to become a facilitator takes skills that may seem to lessen the role of the teacher. However, the facilitator must maintain the learning environment in such a way as to promote learning of material that is a part of the curriculum but using different methods and allowing students to have a role in determining what those methods will be. Tylee and Litt (n.d., p. 19) state:

> The role of the teacher is diverse and has several orientations. One important aspect is that of facilitator of student learning. The facilitator attempts to provide circumstances that will enable students to engage with the learning opportunities and construct for themselves their understandings and skills. This role will interact with those of teacher as learner, colleague and community partner.

The role of the teacher, then, becomes not one who just supplies knowledge (although this may occur), but leads, guides, direct, and supports – no small part in the teaching/learning process. The instructor must have knowledge of the content and resources and how to incorporate the curricular goals into the learners' projected learning activities. There must be communication among teachers and learners; the activities must be agreed upon as means to attain goals; there must be mutual respect for opposing ideas; and there needs to be willingness among all parties to share, reflect and consider all sides.

As in all learning, there should be an informal analysis of students' potential for the heutagogical approach. Powell and Kusuma-Powell (2011, p. 24) note the importance of getting to know students.

Developing an in-depth understanding of each learner enables teachers to

1. Create a psychologically safe environment for every learner.
2. Determine each student's readiness for learning.
3. Identify multiple access points to the curriculum to increase engagement and success.
4. Develop and demonstrate greater emotional intelligence in the classroom.

This is particularly important when using approaches such as heutagogy that may be unfamiliar to the students. For students who do not work well in groups and/or independently or have difficulty sharing their thoughts, this approach may not be suitable.

Grabe and Grabe (1998) state that the student role in the traditional classroom is one in which the student shares information; that is, the student learns; the student shares either through assessments, student-to-teacher or student-to-student. The teacher's role is to present information and manage the classroom. Further, the content is basic literacy with higher-level skills building on lower-level skills that emphasize breadth of knowledge, fact retention, fragmented knowledge and disciplinary separation. Socially, the students use technology independently for drill and practice and direct instruction, and they are assessed on fact retention using traditional tests.

In comparison, the heutagogical learning environment stresses self-determined learning with teachers as facilitators who empower student learning and provide resources for them. The content is meaningful with purposeful learning experiences which are relevant to learners' needs. Socially, students are independent as well as collaborative learners. Technology facilitates exploration, collaboration and self-actualization. Assessments are often self-diagnostic and depend on knowledge application (Eberle and Childress, 2006).

E-learning has been shown to be as effective as face-to-face learning. However, as Clark (2005) notes,

> Having participated in many poor training sessions in the classroom and on the computer, we recognize that it's not the medium that causes learning. Rather it is the design of the lesson itself and the best use of instructional methods that make the difference. A learner-centered approach suggests that we design lessons that accommodate human learning processes regardless of the media involved. (p. 6)

In other words, teachers do not play a less significant role; they play a different role and it is one that is at the heart of good teaching. As more has been learned about education and learning, teachers, for the most part, have adapted their skills to suit the needs of students to help them learn in the best ways possible. Heutagogy enables growth for instructor and student alike.

Originally, andragogy, the precursor to heutagogy, was identified with adult learning, and many assumed that to be the case for heutagogy. However, if one studies the skills and outcomes of heutagogy, it becomes apparent that heutagogy is an approach that should be available to learners of all ages. Hase and Kenyon (2000) claim that heutagogy, may be viewed as a natural progression from earlier educational methodologies – in particular from capability development – and may well provide the optimal approach to learning in the twenty-first century. Stephenson and Weil (1992) describe *capable people* as those who know how to learn; are creative; have a high degree of self-efficacy; can apply competencies in novel as well as familiar situations; and can work well with others. In a global world in which citizens must come together to solve global problems, surely we need to start at an early age to groom them to become effectively capable.

Students need to have their thinking channelled into creative problem solving before, as Ken Robinson (2009, p. 16) points out, education stifles, 'the individual talents and abilities of too many students and kills their motivation to learn'. His view is that students begin their school careers unafraid to be creative but the demands for testing and conformity do not allow students to become all they can be. He asserts that we, 'need to rethink the basic nature of human ability and the basic purposes of education' (p. 17). Heutagogy allows for freedom of thought, original ideas and the opportunity to enrich learning by active participation – not just rote memorization and stilted lessons. When children are first in school, for the most part, they are not afraid to take risks and will blurt out ideas and answers as soon as they think them. Later they become not only self-conscious just because they are going through personal changes, they also become less willing to risk a 'wrong' answer even though their thinking may be quite clear. No longer is it possible for the teacher to teach everything; students must take responsibility for learning, as well, and approach learning creatively and with enthusiasm. The main reason for students to drop out of school is lack of interest. And lack of interest is often the result of their not being allowed to express creative problem-solving skills. Rather than assuming there is one way to solve a problem, students should be allowed to explore, think and develop alternative solutions. Capable adults can do this. A heutagogical approach can provide the direction.

So, how do facilitators encourage students to become more self-determined learners? First, there must be an atmosphere of trust. Students must feel that their thoughts and ideas will be taken seriously and not be maligned as irrelevant or foolish. Everyone's opinion must be included in conversations. Teachers and students should be viewed as partners who work together, share ideas and resources and are open to constructive criticism. Work should be seen as a collaborative effort. If there is to be effective teamwork among peers, the following tenets suggested by Clark (2005, p. 8) should be adhered to:

1. Foster mutual respect for the expertise of all team members.
2. Help weaker team members believe that their effort is vital to team success.
3. Support a shared belief in the cooperative capabilities of the team.
4. Hold individual team members accountable for their contributions to the team effort.
5. Direct the team's competitive spirit outside the team and the organization.

All members of a learning team should feel that they are as important to the process as everyone else and should expect to contribute to the efforts. Teachers should point out that there is room for both leaders and followers but that all should prepare to contribute. It may be wise for the teacher to remind students that good leaders do not take over a project but, rather, they work to ensure that each participant has a role. Students who are more likely to be followers will not be allowed to sit back while others make decisions and carry out plans. They may not see themselves as leaders, but they are equally important in the success of the tasks at hand. Students should also be aware that the team as a whole is reflected in a project's success or failure. And, while competitiveness may be a factor in the motivation of students to do their best, this should be a factor only as teams against teams – not team members versus team members. Healthy competition can be good for motivation; too much competitive spirit may work against the common goal. These tenets bring up an important question about learning: What about e-learning? Is collaboration effective in e-learning projects? The answer is, yes. With the current social media, virtual drop-boxes and e-mail, students can collaborate online as well as, if not more advantageously, than face-to-face. Students in face-to-face classes may need to physically meet to solve problems which can be difficult with class, work and personal schedules. Online, students may work synchronously or asynchronously to achieve their goals. The nature of social media is that it is active. Students who participate do not do so passively. They share and respond, they act and react. Alley and Jansek (2001, pp. 5–6) list ten characteristics of good quality online learning that fit well with self-directed, student empowered learning.

1. Knowledge is constructed, not transmitted.
2. Students can take full responsibility for their own learning.
3. Students are motivated to want to learn.
4. The course provides 'mental white space' for reflection.
5. Learning activities appropriately match student learning styles.
6. Experiential, active learning augments the website environment.
7. Solitary and interpersonal learning activities are interspersed.
8. Inaccurate prior learning is identified and corrected.
9. 'Spiral learning' provides for revisiting and expanding prior lessons.
10. The master teacher is able to guide the overall learning process.

Alley and Jansek (2001, p. 3) go on to assert that, 'It is apparent that learning communities require more than just well-designed instruction. They also involve strategic, ongoing efforts by the instructor to encourage student-to-student interaction, as well as student-to-instructor interaction, and to have students get to know each other as learners and as people. They are communities in the truest, most culture-based sense of the word.'

One can argue that no matter what the platform – face-to-face or e-learning, heutagogy will be a theory whose application can result in benefits for learners. However, heutagogy is not the only way to teach. As noted earlier, the instruction needs to fit the learning, the content and the learners' capabilities. For example, we need to consider students with varying abilities or challenges. By incorporating the tenets of Universal Design for Learning (UDL), heutagogy becomes a force for all. Universal Design for Learning (UDL) is defined by the National Center on Universal Design for Learning (2012, p. 1) as, 'a set of principles for curriculum development that give all individuals equal opportunities to learn'. The three basic ideas behind UDL are:

1. Multiple means of representation (Presenting information and content in different ways)
2. Multiple means of expression (Differentiating ways that students can express what they know)
3. Multiple means of engagement (stimulating interest and motivation for learning). (p. 4)

By incorporating these ideas into a heutagogical approach, most students will find success. Figure 10.2 demonstrates the relationship of heutagogy with its double-loop learning and UDL along with the concepts of collaboration and problem solving, two skill sets that according to Pink (2005) are needed for global learning.

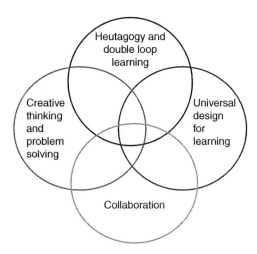

Figure 10.2 The relationship among heutagogy, UDL, collaboration and creative thinking and problem solving.

UDL should be a given in any classroom. It is a logical, common-sense way to provide inclusion for as many students as possible. Whether students have varied abilities or learning preferences, UDL will address the diverse needs of students.

Using a heutagogical approach requires planning and monitoring by the teacher; however, this doesn't have to be an overwhelming task. If educators think through what it is they expect from the students in terms of process and product, and they are flexible in their thinking and expectations (after all, students may want to pursue goals from a different but acceptable angle) the rest should be fairly straightforward. The teacher facilitates; he/she does not dictate. Table 10.2 offers an example of how one may plan for a heutagogical approach to teaching the solar system.

Whether or not one uses this type of template or designs another, there are benefits to having a diagram to go by although after practice, this will become less necessary. This can work well for projects across the curriculum. Imagine music students who are learning about great composers and their works or English students delving into the history of a genre and comparing and contrasting it to others. The influences of events in a particular country over the culture of that country could be a theme for social studies. Math could be studied through the changes in technology. The possibilities are endless for thoughtful problem solving using heutagogy. Melinda Kolk offers the following idea for hard-to-reach learners (2011, p. 6):

> Students could create mock social network pages for characters they are studying or elements on the periodic table. How might Socrates comment on A current YouTube video? How would Plato?

Others could write about events in the style of various periodicals such as *Time Magazine* or as newscasts.

Blaschke (2012, p. 27) makes an important point when she states that, 'Instructors not only must change their approach to teaching and learning, but also ensure that they explain this type of learning to their students from the very start of class'. While the process can be introduced early in the school years, for adults who have been used to traditional types of teaching and learning, there may be a larger learning curve and greater paradigm shift. Well-managed classes with instructors who are comfortable as facilitators and are empathetic

Table 10.2 Template for heutagogical teaching of the solar system

Project/lesson title: What Should the Future of Space Travel Be ?			
Goal(s): Students will learn about the solar system. Students will present arguments about future of space travel.			
Problem: Given what we know about our solar system. is space travel necessary and viable for the future?			
Performance Objective(s)	After the project is completed, the students will be able to... 1. Name the eight planets in order from the sun on a quiz with 100% accuracy. 2. Identify other specified objects in the sky. 3. List reasons why space travel is necessary/not necessary and whether or not if is viable for the future. 4. State what they learned, how it changed their thinking, and why it is improtant		
Activities	1. Research and determine what area of solar system to study based on, but not limited to suggested list	2. Initial planning with group and teacher Decide how to proceed and what will be needed to complete project	3. Present and defend solution to problem. Reflect on project and outcomes. Suggest future areas of study.
Collaboration Plan	Groups of four/ heterogeneous groups	Students determine how to set up group dynamics (leader? Reporter? Etc.)	Every student to participate and be engaged in project
UDL plan	Multiple Representation Gather facts from multiple sources use primary sources, Internet, books, visuals, field trips, etc.	Multiple Means of Action/ Expression Students may prepare materials using PowerPoint, Perzi, Glogster, Charts, Posters, Drawings, Models	Multiple Means of Engagement Students may arrange for speakers, field trips, computer use, video equipment, recordings, etc.

Table 10.2 Continued

Heutagogy Plan	Teacher	Students
	1. Provide multiple resources and opportunities including visuals, texts, software, field trips, examples, information and practive for debating/ defending work 2. Answer questions, provide examples, monitor progress of groups and individuals 3. Lead discussion following each day's project work to determine progress, time management, and success of collaboration 4. Provide clear instructions for both collaboration, presentation, audience expectations, and product 5. Model reflection	1. Use multiple resources and opportunities as fit the project and group/ individual's needs 2. Question others; reflect on answers; apply or do not; keep track of progress 3. Contribute to daily reflective discussion. Provide positive suggestions and constructive criticism. 4. Follow instructions but collaborate with teacher for any deviations. 5. Learn to reflect, debate, provide sound arguments with support for ideas.
Materials	Primary sources Texts, Newspapers and other media, Internet, paper, Materials to build models if needed	Students may request additional materials
Assessments	**Formative** 1. Informal observations to monitor work habits and progress 2. Daily reflective discussions to determine successes and concems 3. Individual and group meetings to determine knowledge and skills being learned 4. Journaling (text or pictorally)	**Summative** 1. Quiz over planets and other objects in space. 2. Presentation by group of findings and ideas for solution to problem including ability to defend and debate solution 3. Reflection paper/drawing/ oral report to teacher concerning individual success/failure/change in beliefs/new ideas, etc.

Rubric

Points	1	2	3	4	5
Name eight planets in order from sun out	Named two planets	Named four planets	Named six planets	Named eight planets but not in order	Named all planets in order from sun out
Identify and describe ten types of objects in space	Named and described 2 objects,	Named and accurately described 3–4 objects	Named and accurately described 5–6 objects	Named and accurately described 7–8 objects	Named and accurately described 10 objects
List reasons for/against space exploration	Listed why would like to travel in space	Listed 1 reason for space exploring. No support	Listed 2–3 reasons for space exploration Included some support	Listed 3–4 reasons for/against space exploration Included accurate support	Listed five reasons for/against spaced exploration Included accurated support
Group presentation	Group was not prepared; No visuals Support for position very weak	Group was somewhat prepared; Visuals did not support material; Support for position was weak.	Group was prepared for presentation but visuals were poorly prepared Support for position was clear but not strong.	Group was prepared but lacked organization Defense of position supported Visuals included	Group was prepared; had accurated facts; Presentation was clear; defense of position was strong. Visuals included
Reflection	Few journal entries; paper itemized what was done.	Journal had many missing entries; paper not reflective	Journal missing some entries; paper not reflective	Journal up-to-date; reflection paper did not include all items to be addressed	Kept journal up-to-date; Reflection paper thorough and complete

to their students' apprehensions will breed greater success. According to Eberle and Childress (2006, p. 12),

> Heutagogy is not for the feint of heart or lazy of mind. Instructors must be facilitators who have the confidence to be able to let go of the ownership of learning. Rigidly structured environments are not conducive to heutagogy. Heutagogy does allow instructors and students alike to be creative and to enjoy a mutual respect of ideas … In a world of rapidly evolving information, heutagogy can be the catalyst for students to explore avenues of learning in ways that help them to be capable people who are prepared for their roles in society.

References

Alley, L. and Jansek, K. (2001), 'The ten keys to quality assurance and assessment in online learning', *Journal of Interactive Instructional Development*, 13(3), 3–18.

Argyris, C. (n.d.), *Theories of Learning in Educational Psychology, Chris Argyris: Double Loop Learning*. Retrieved 9 May 2012 from: www.lifecircles-inc.com/Learningtheories/constructivism/argyris.html.

Blaschke, L. M. (2012), 'Heutagogy and lifelong learning: a review of heutagogical practice and self-determined learning', *The International Review of Research in Open and Distance Learning*. Retrieved 4 May 2012 from: www.irrodl.org/index.php/irrodl/article/view/1076.

Clark, R. E. (2005), *Research-tested Team Motivation Strategies*. Retrieved 30 March 2012 from: www.cogtech.usc.edu/publications/clark_team_motivation.pdf.

Eberle, J. H. and Childress, M. D. (2006), 'Heutagogy: it isn't your mother's pedagogy any more', *National Social Science Journal,* 28(1), 28–32.

Grabe. M. & Grabe C. (1998), *Integrating Technology for Meaningful Learning*. New York: Houghton Mifflin.

Hase, S. and Kenyon, K. (2000), 'From andragogy to heutagogy', Retrieved 29 April 2004 from: http://ultibase.rmit.edu.au/Articles/dec00/hase2.htm.

Kolk, M. (2011), 'Connecting with hard-to-reach learners', *Creative Educator*. San Diego: Tech4Learning.

Knowles, M. (1984), *The Adult Learner: A Neglected Species*. Houston: GulfPublishing.

National Center on Universal Design for Learning (2012), Retrieved 8 May 2012 from: www.udlcenter.org/aboutudl/whatisudl.

Pink, D. (2005), *A Whole New Mind*. New York: Riverhead Books.

Powell, W. and Kusuma-Powell, O. (2011), *How to Teach Now, Five Keys to Personalized Learning in the Global Classroom*. Alexandria, VA: ASCD.

Robinson, K. (2009), *The Element*. New York: Penguin.

Stephenson, J. and Weil, S. (1992), *Quality in Learning: A Capability Approach in Higher Education*. London: Kogan Page.

Tylee, J. & MLitt (n.d.), *Teacher as Facilitator: One of the face-to-face Teacher's Roles*. Retrieved 5 May 2012 from: www.education4skills.com/jtylee/teacher_as_facilitator.html.

11

Learner Defined Learning

Stewart Hase

Summary

In this chapter I describe how heutagogy can be used to deliver exciting training programmes that place the learner at the heart of the learning experience. Some of the principles of Systems Thinking (Emery and Trist, 1965) and, more specifically, the Search Conference Technique (Emery and Purser, 1996; Weisbord, 1992) and heutagogy are combined to provide potentially exciting training programmes. I have been using this approach for a while (Hase, 2010), in both the public and private sectors, using an action learning and reflective practice to hone the approach. Despite fears to the contrary, the approach can also be used where there is a need for participants to achieve very specific competencies and knowledge, and where very structured assessment methods are applied. What the facilitator of this hybrid of systems thinking and heutagogy needs to do is to really know their subject matter, be quick on their feet and be skilled at small group techniques.

The training context

There is a considerable industry in conducting accredited and non-accredited training programmes for the public and private sectors. Traditionally this has been delivered face-to-face although online offerings for training are becoming increasingly popular, as they have the advantages of cost savings, convenience and a new generation of employees who use the ever-evolving communications technology as second nature. The training programme may be designed in conjunction with the employer for specific outcomes or can be provided as an 'off the shelf' package with perhaps contextual tinkering to increase its relevance.

The trainer (teacher) largely determines the 'what' and 'how' of learning, which is, in essence, the curriculum, although this may be described in different ways. So, we may refer to competencies, the programme, needs, the process, training outcomes and so on.

For a few years I have been experimenting with using methods based on heutagogy in short training programmes of between half a day and three days in length. I have also incorporated some of the philosophy and techniques from systems thinking and the search conference (Emery and Purser, 1996; Emery and Trist, 1965; Weisbord, 1992). The search conference is a systematic approach to strategic planning that has been used in a wide variety of organizational and community settings. The objective is, as much as possible, to involve the whole system (organization), or at least a representation of the whole organization, in the process and then, using a prescribed set of techniques that are essentially democratic in nature, determine the required actions.

The search conference is an open systems approach that forces the participants to think of their organization/community as a system that operates in an environment of other systems that have an impact on them. In comparison a closed system is inward looking and is not concerned, to its detriment, with the ever-changing external environment. I like to think of heutagogy as aligned with open systems thinking by taking into account readiness to change.

My approach has been to involve the training participants at the commencement of the workshop in planning and negotiating the content, the learning experience and, if necessary, the assessment. Initially, this involves revealing the proposed agenda and outcomes as established by the employer. Small groups of around six people are formed using a nominal group technique to ensure a good mix and prevent 'group think'. Using flip-chart paper and coloured pens, the small groups are asked a series of questions that depend a little on the context but usually concern: the extent to which the group agree or disagree with the objectives of the course; where they disagree, to spell out the reasons and what they would like to change; the actual learning needs of the group with respect to the general content area; any contextual issues that are important; what questions they have; desired outcomes; and how they would like to see the course conducted. The groups then report back on their deliberations and the flip chart paper is hung from the walls for continued reference. The groups then take a break and I design the programme based on this information. In some cases I undertake this design phase with the involvement of the group depending on the number of participants and the potential difficulty of the task.

Clearly, the extent of the initial questions and the time given to them depends on the size of the group, the length of the course and the course intent. The general aim is the same, nonetheless, to design a course relevant to the participants, taking into account their current levels of knowledge and skills. At regular intervals through the course I ask participants what new questions they have about the subject and whether there is a need to change direction with content or process. If necessary, course adjustments are made. From a heutagogical perspective the objective is to keep track of participants' learning and their changing needs to ensure learner-centredness and to increase the potential for learning as we described in Chapter 2.

The course design can vary a great deal. Groups or pairs sometimes form around specific interests and preferences for how they wish to undertake their learning. Using the resources provided and what they can find on the internet, for example, these groups report back to the other participants at specified times. This reporting is critical to ensuring that knowledge, skills and learning are transferred to others and are open for discussion and analysis. Sometimes the whole group decides to pursue various activities and discussions without necessarily breaking up into smaller units. The facilitator might provide advice about what activities can be undertaken, videos to watch and so on. Most discussions, activities and analyses, however, are undertaken in small groups with feedback in plenary sessions.

For those who are intent on ensuring specific content is delivered, I ensure that all participants receive a copy of essential resource materials at the beginning of the programme. My experience has been that people can read just as well as I can, and that my repeating material orally is not very useful, and that lecturing in general is not at all effective in promoting knowledge and skills acquisition, or indeed, intelligent thought (see, e.g. Bligh, 1972).

If a course is to involve more than one day, I try to convince the employer to have a gap of at least two weeks between training days. This enables participants to practice new skills and to return to the training with new, perhaps more relevant, questions. This is in keeping with heutagogical principles and is also in accord with what we know about behaviour change strategies used in well-recognized methods such as cognitive behaviour psychology; the same strategies are used effectively in psychotherapy, coaching and action learning.

The search conference approach was adapted from a process used by Alan Davies who applied it in the 1970s (e.g. Davies, 1977, 1979) in an educational context but in curriculum design. In a recent personal communication (Hase, 2011) Davies explained that at that time, other educators and administrators were unhappy with what they thought to be an anarchic and inappropriate process. However, participants, after initially experiencing some anxiety, enjoyed the experience and achieved what Davies considered were excellent outcomes (Hase, 2011).

In the early 1990s Davies used the search conference approach in the classroom with a group of doctoral students in Singapore (Sankaran et al., 2007). These students were mostly from engineering or other scientific disciplines and were undertaking research using action research. Action research is firmly grounded in social science and qualitative methods and hence was rather alien to the students. Davies was teaching the students action research. He used the same search conference technique to conduct the programme on the grounds that the students: knew more about research methods than he did; could read the required texts and readings as well as he could; that his role was helping them negotiate the content and the doctoral process (which he knew a lot about); and that context was the most important learning consideration and required facilitation not teaching. The approach appeared to be successful (Sankaran et al., 2007).

A case in point

I was recently asked to conduct a workshop about change management for a group within a fairly large public sector organization. The brief for the workshop was relatively simple and the request was for standard change management strategies to be delivered to about 12 people in a two-day workshop. The background given was that the organization had decided to implement a new quality system and had appointed a team to undertake quality reviews. Apparently the implementation had not gone well and the response was to assist the quality reviewers to gain skills in managing the change process.

Using a heutagogical approach the workshop started with the usual introduction and an ice-breaker that I often use involving the use of lots of different coloured Play Dough (a malleable substance like dough that can be easily moulded into whatever size and shape one wants). Participants are asked to make whatever they like with the Play Dough, but it must say something about themselves that the others in the team do not know. Participants can be as creative or as uncreative as they like, depending on their whim. They are then asked to place their creations on a table in such a way that represents the communication within the team: a simple sociogram. So, Joy places her item close to Joe but a long way from Barry because she communicates more with Joe. Sally puts herself close to Barry and near to Joe and so on. The process usually involves some to-ing and fro-ing and good-natured banter. Then we talk about the creations and the sociogram. Obviously there are many useful insights gained from this exercise and it starts the creative juices flowing.

Next, we used a simple technique from search conferencing where nominal groups are formed around tables: there were three groups of four in this case. Small groups help prevent group-think and dilute the influence of power. The employer's intent of the workshop was spelled out by the group's team leader: I had briefed the team leader for this task beforehand. Each table was given some flip-chart paper and lots of coloured pens for recording their thoughts. The groups were asked to undertake several tasks and given 15 minutes to complete:

- The extent to which they agreed or disagreed with the intent of the workshop.
- What they thought the workshop should be about and their understanding of the problem of managing change.
- What should be covered by the workshop that would really make a difference to solving the problem.
- Their current level of skill in the area of change.
- What they would like to have learned or be better at, at the end of the two days.

A member of each group then presented the outcomes of their deliberations in a plenary session and all the sheets of flip-chart paper were left on the walls. Discussion and clarification of the findings was encouraged. At the same time I collated a list of the learning needs on a whiteboard. I then asked the participants to prioritize their learning needs. Each person was given five coloured dots, sticky on one side, to use. They could place five on one learning need or three on one and two on another, or five single dots on five different needs depending on their personal importance. This resulted in a prioritized list.

Normally I would then have called a break and undertaken the programme design, however, what was clear from the participants' output and subsequent discussion was that their needs were not at all about change management. Rather, it was about dealing with a problematic and still evolving quality system, poor communication, working in a stressful situation in which the group was being treated as pariahs by other staff whose work they had to review, managing feelings, managing upwards, dealing with difficult people and poor implementation of the quality checking system. This information completely changed the agenda for the remainder of the two days. Throughout the workshop I constantly reviewed the skill needs of the group and changed course whenever it was clear that needs had changed. The new skills enabled the team to develop a change action plan with some very specific, and in some cases quite individual skills, tactics and strategies to implement. Each person decided how they would evaluate their performance on their plan by the next session in a few weeks time and committed to keeping a diary to record their efforts.

If I had not taken this approach and delivered a change management 'course' designed around what the employer thought should be delivered I am sure there would have been little motivation and little learning. The feedback from the groups was very positive. A subsequent workshop to follow-up on their action plans demonstrated an improvement in skills and increased confidence.

Although such dramatic a shift in focus may happen infrequently, dealing with even minor shifts in emphasis at the beginning and throughout the programme are critical to maintaining motivation and ensuring relevant learning. I receive considerable feedback from participants that this approach is exciting and provides an opportunity for them to pursue areas of need and interest. More importantly, participants have a sense of ownership and increased commitment due to the democratic nature of the approach.

Not all training workshops are 'free wheeling' where assessment of competencies or some other outcome is not a requirement. In cases involving assessment there is usually a part of the 'curriculum' that is fixed and cannot be ignored. Nonetheless, the same technique can be used and may, in fact, be more important. The approach provides an opportunity to find out about current experience and skills, learning styles, specific questions and, more importantly, learning needs. Again, it is critical to continuously evaluate how the learning, skills and learning needs have shifted during the programme. Thus, the emphasis is formative rather than summative.

Recently I asked a group of about 120 trainers involved in a large rural fire fighting service in Australia how they would go about training a group of fire fighters to use a new fire engine. The picture I had was one of an appliance from the mid-1800s but they understood what I was asking. They described how they would probably show some pictures or videos of the machine in action, go through the manual, go over the fire engine and explain all its parts, demonstrate how to use it and then have the group practice until competent.

I then asked the group what would happen if we put the manual on the seat of the new fire truck and left them to it. Their role would be to linger around and make sure that nothing untoward happened and provide advice if the learning group got stuck. It was decided that given that many of the groups would have had experience with fire engines, even if it was varied and some did not, that they would probably work it out for themselves. Some would read the manual and others would tinker. They would learn from each other and perhaps from the facilitator who would be just one of the groups. These fire service trainers conceded that they would probably also learn a thing or two. Everyone would become competent, some before others, and in different ways.

There is nothing necessarily unique in this approach but it does contain many of the elements of heutagogy and certainly demonstrates learner managed learning. More than anything, this approach displays confidence in the ability of people to learn in the way that they are probably hard wired to do from birth.

Reflections and issues

The facilitator

I have found this approach to conducting training to be immensely satisfying from the perspective of the facilitator. However, preparation is crucial to success. There is no doubt that I have to be really on top of my subject area because there is no possibility of prompting by using PowerPoint slides.

I usually take along reading material and references to other reading and websites. Accessibility to the internet during a workshop is not usually a problem and is useful for activities. It helps if the group can read some materials beforehand, although the response to this requirement is variable. My laptop is full of video clips and other resources that can be accessed during the training course, all of which can be found in a pre-prepared folder. I also have available a number of potential experiential activities to call upon depending on the programme design.

While this may sound like 'flying by the seat of the pants', it rarely feels like this assuming one has a very good grasp of content and concepts. Context and application seem to be the main issues and they are driven by the learner. Recently I was explaining this approach to a group of trainers and it occurred to me that it is not unlike management coaching, except to a group rather than an individual. Management coaching involves focusing on the specific needs of the person being coached, determining appropriate action, supporting change and evaluating progress, in a cyclical manner. The coach is not expected to have all the answers but is a powerhouse of resources and knowing about how to learn and change.

Initially, using this approach can involve some anxiety and it always requires a fair degree of enthusiasm and energy. However, the knowledge that participants may learn something really useful and be exposed to more than just a 'memory dump' can be a great driving factor.

The facilitator needs to develop skills in managing groups using a Socratic rather than a directive technique. This might involve deconstructing problems, exploration, reflection and analysis. In fact being able to ask questions and get others to do the same is at the heart of heutagogy.

As a facilitator I find that I have, more often or not, to compromise with regard to assessment. Where competency attainment is concerned, the assessment process is often fixed. Nonetheless I find it possible to be a little flexible with the timing of the assessment, using participants to coach others and injecting higher-order assessment as an add-on for those who are asking more challenging questions.

The client and the participants

Clients vary somewhat in their capacity to embrace heutagogy, or at least the approach that I suggest. The most anxious people are those who are used to having a detailed run sheet that covers just about every minute of their day. Fortunately, this sort of compulsive behaviour is relatively rare. Most managers in organizations have little experience in education and the prevalent model they have to base their experience on is highly teacher-centric and is one in which the learner is a passive recipient. The learner-centred approach can be a little daunting and appears to be anarchic to the uninitiated. It is important to reassure the anxious client that there is indeed structure in the apparent chaos and that desired outcomes will be achieved, albeit in a different way than might be expected. Many clients take the advice and eagerly watch what happens.

Participant reactions are generally very positive. As I have reported elsewhere (Hase, 2011, p. 6), 'Most participants state that they find the process: engaging and motivating; that it provides an opportunity for dealing with real, rather than assumed, problems; flexible by providing an opportunity to follow areas of real interest and need as they become apparent during the program; relevant; and empowering.'

Early anxiety due to the apparent lack of structure dissipates once participants become involved in the group activities and groups become task focused. Any preference for working as an individual, in pairs or in groups can be met once we have agreed on the workshop objectives and how they are to be achieved. Groups find being able to determine how to go about achieving the course outcomes to be very refreshing. Some groups do decide to stick together, although I nearly always break them into smaller units depending on specific context, interest and the questions raised. Each of the groups is responsible for feeding back their discussion to the rest of the groups and are asked to record their findings on flip-chart paper or using technology. Information dissemination can involve simple exposition. A gallery walk is a fun approach in which groups walk around the presentations and ask questions of the presenters. I have also found techniques such as the 'Knowledge Café' to be very effective in disseminating information among the group. The more adventurous might try variations of Open Space Technology as a means to getting ideas and issues out on the table as they are discussed. However, it is important to make sure participants know how to use these approaches.

Conclusion

My experimenting with this approach continues, and I continue to marvel at how a dynamic environment can be quickly created when people are given control over their own learning. I am confident that as we continue to experiment, new techniques will evolve to make learning more effective and more relevant.

References

Bligh, D. (1972), *What's the Use of Lectures?* London: Penguin.

Davies, A. T. (1977), 'An alternative general studies curriculum: a description, results and evaluation', *ACT Papers on Education,* Canberra, 83–91.

—. (1979), 'Application of participative planning to Trade Union Training, community involvement in schooling and Secondary College courses'. Paper presented at the *Innovations Proceedings of AAAE Innovations Conference,* Canberra, April.

Emery, F. and Trist, E. (1965), 'The causal texture of organisations', *Human Relations,* 18, 21–32.

Emery, M. and Purser, R. E. (1996), *The Search Conference: A Powerful Method for Planning Organizational Change and Community Action.* San Francisco, CA: Jossey-Bass.

Hase, S. (2010), 'Learner defined curriculum: heutagogy and action learning in vocational training', *Southern Institute of Technology Journal of Applied Research*, Special Edition on Action Research. Retrieved 2 November 2012 from: http://sitjar.sit.ac.nz.

Sankaran, S., Hase, S., Dick, B. and Davies, A. T. (2007), 'Singing different tunes from the same song sheet: four perspectives of teaching the doing of action research', *Action Learning: Research and Practice,* 5(3), 293–30.

Weisbord, M. R. (ed.) (1992), *Discovering Common Ground: How Future Search Conferences Bring People Together to Achieve Breakthrough Innovation, Empowerment, Shared Vision, and Collaborative Action.* San Francisco, CA: Berrett-Koehler.

12

Practitioner Development in Early Years Education

Natalie Canning

Summary

This chapter is based on a research project involving case studies from early years practitioners, working with children 0–5 years old. The participants were studying a module to complete their degree and achieve the Early Years Professional Status (EYPS). They all lived and worked in England, as EYPS is a status only recognized in that country; the participants had chosen to study through a distance-learning programme. The chapter considers the impact that studying for EYPS has had on professional identity and personal empowerment and the extent to which participants were able to adopt a paradigm of heutagogy or self-determined learning (Hase and Kenyon, Chapter 2, this volume).

The case studies explore how participants are motivated and empowered to apply their learning to their own practice and to influence other early years practitioners. Through engaging with heutagogic or self-determined learning strategies, the research considers the extent to which participants were successful in influencing a shift in thinking within themselves and in those with whom they work. All participants recognized not only the emotional energy they invested in their personal learning journey, but also the importance of building their knowledge and understanding, and then disseminating their learning within their workplace to support children's early experiences. Finally, I explore key themes from the case studies in how a programme of study can support personal and professional transitions to influence change and continuing professional development through self-determined learning. The names of people who took part in the research are fictional.

What is the EYPS?

EYPS is a graduate-led programme designed to up-skill the early years workforce in England. It focuses on adults working with children aged 0–5 years in the private, voluntary and independent early years sector. Over the last decade, there has been a drive to improve the quality of early years provision in England and the focus of this, by the UK Labour Government (1997–2010) was on encouraging practitioners to undertake relevant qualifications. For many people this has meant studying for a foundation degree in early years alongside their employment in an early years setting, then completing a 'top up' year to gain a degree. EYPS is achieved after completion of a degree and has several different pathways enabling practitioners to gain the desired status. The required study can take from three months to one year depending on experience and prior qualifications.

The EYPS programme aims to support professional development of early years practitioners and provides formal recognition for their work in leading practice across the English Early Years Foundation Stage (EYFS) curricula. An early years professional (EYP) role is described in the EYPS candidate handbook in the following terms:

> Early Years Professionals will be key to raising the quality of early years provision. They will be change agents to improve practice. They will be expected to lead practice across the EYFS in a range of settings, modelling the skills and behaviours that promote good outcomes for children and supporting and mentoring other practitioners. (CWDC, 2007, p. 4)

The government made a commitment to professionalizing the early years workforce in England by aiming to have an EYP in all children's centres by 2010 and in every full day care setting by 2015. However, in 2010 a new government came into power and although it made a commitment to the professionalism of the early years workforce, all specific targets were removed. The change of government has meant a shift in priorities for the early years sector. In the past, EYPS programmes of study had been fully funded. From 2012 the majority of students have had to self-fund unless they are working in a designated area of deprivation. In 2011, the *Tickell Review* consulted on the Early Years Foundation Stage (EYFS) 0–5 years curricula in England and clearly stated that a graduate workforce in the early years is important (Tickell, 2011). This has meant that EYPS will continue in the short term.

The research

There were two parts to the study: a survey followed by in-depth interviews of a smaller group. The survey involved a cohort of 25 adult students, 24 females and 1 male, with a foundation degree in early years. Participants were aged between 25 and 56, with a minimum of 4 years experience in Early Years education. They were on a 12-month long process that included studying for a 60-credit module to achieve a degree with EYPS through distance education. The students were asked at the six-month point of their course to complete a questionnaire based on their experience of studying a distance learning-based EYPS programme. The questionnaires were anonymous, although the last question asked if they would be interested in taking part in a more detailed study, and to give their contact details. Of the 25, 6 students, all female, agreed to be involved further.

Participants were owners or managers of child car facilities, child minders and room leaders within larger nurseries. All worked in the private, voluntary or independent sector. The six participants took part in a detailed telephone interview lasting between 30 and 40 minutes. The interviews were undertaken in the ninth month of the course and after students had completed their setting visit at the end of the programme. The interviews were undertaken by the author, and were semi-structured, open-ended and encouraged participants to discuss issues about their experiences during the course.

The questionnaire investigated two overarching questions:

- How have you kept motivated through your study?
- How has your study for EYPS affected your confidence?

The in-depth telephone interviews asked detailed questions about personal learning journeys on the programme and the benefits and challenges of the experience. From these questions the reoccurring themes of reflection and personal empowerment emerged. It was also apparent that each of the participants had made an emotional investment in undertaking the programme of study and seeing it through to the end.

Emotional investment

According to the tenets of heutagogy learning is a highly individual process with unpredictable effects when it occurs. Any educational experience needs to recognize this complexity (Hase and Kenyon, Chapter 2, this volume). Controlling the factors that interface with the cognitive activity is also critical. The emotional investment that the student makes is one such factor evident in this study.

Enrolling on a programme of study means that, to a considerable extent, a person is prepared to invest time, energy and possibly make a financial commitment, into learning. What is sometimes unexpected is the amount of emotional energy that is invested along the way. It is not always apparent to the learner that they spend a considerable amount of time thinking about their study, worrying about assessment or, perhaps more commonly, feeling anxious about their progress. Gradually the programme of study is subsumed into daily life, adding to the roles and responsibilities that already exist. Ashton and Elliott (2007) suggest that it is difficult to separate learning from everyday events and, therefore, it becomes intertwined with all the other activities that fill days, weeks, evenings, weekends and even years. However, what is apparent is that although a level of emotional investment in learning is inevitable, the intensity of it fluctuates depending on the different pressure points of the programme or with other events that are happening at the same time. Consequently, it is possible to identify when emotional intensity may occur, for example around assessment and then develop strategies to cope with it.

Recognizing the triggers that influence an emotional response in learning is important because it requires personal reflection about individual learning strategies, consistent with heutagogical principles. These strategies will be different for each individual student and will hold significant meaning and relevance for their personal learning journey. The emotional investment that a student makes involves a complex set of reasons and circumstances that is highly individual and requires unique intervention. Learning requires flexible mechanisms which can support the student to self-direct and self-motivate their learning, while providing an environment where students can ask for help. For students, acknowledging emotional investment means engaging with personal reflection. Annabel, a child minder reflected:

> I didn't realise how much the course would cost me in emotional terms, I went
> from feeling anxious about whether I was ready to undertake EYPS and whether

my practice was good enough, to then worrying about it all of the time, because I couldn't find the time to devote to completing the work for the final setting visit. Because it was distance learning and because I work by myself most of the time, I sometimes felt isolated, but had to remind myself to use my mentor and connect with other members of the course online. I had to find ways to deal with my emotional roller-coaster and about half way through, I seemed to lurch from crisis to crisis, but in the end, and I realised this as I talked in my final interview on the final setting visit, 'yes, I am worthy of this, I'm good at what I do and I deserve recognition for all of my hard work and years of experience'. It was quite a liberating feeling!

The beginnings of empowerment

The questionnaires showed that the majority of the students were motivated to study, but found it difficult to fit the study around other demands such as family and work. Generally there was anxiety in relation to being able to complete the programme and being able to 'sell' themselves at the final setting visit assessment. The interviews provided an opportunity to explore these issues in much more detail.

Annabel's reflection on her learning journey demonstrates how her engagement with her own approach to learning or heutagogic strategies to continue to study, even through the pressure points of the programme, supported a sense of personal empowerment. Empowerment is an imprecise concept, being subject to individual interpretation and dependent upon usually long-held values and beliefs (Gomm, 1993). For an individual, it can sometimes be difficult to recognize when achieving a sense of personal empowerment happens, and the difference that achieving it makes. Empowerment can sometimes relate to the gaining of recognition for one's achievement, the completion of study and gaining status. However, perhaps more significant but less recognized, is the process of empowerment, fulfilled by engaging with new or different ideas, having the confidence to explore them in practice and reflecting on the personal and professional impact. Rivera and Tharp (2006) consider empowerment to go beyond an individual and emerge through interaction with others and in a wider community. For early years practitioners this empowerment begins with talking to colleagues, making small changes and reflecting on the significance for children's learning and development. Personal empowerment starts when there is a capacity for seeing beyond the immediate challenges and starting to imagine the possibilities.

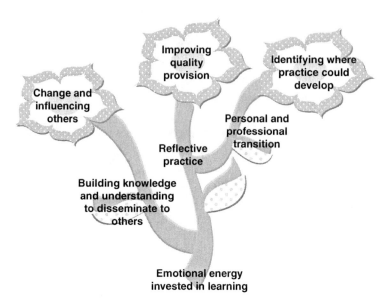

Figure 12.1 Empowerment and heutagogy.

The flower diagram (Figure 12.1) illustrates how personal empowerment develops beyond the initial idea of engaging with heutagogy and how heutagogic strategies for learning may support a capacity for change.

Reflective practice

Reflective practice is essential once an investment to learning has been made. As mentioned in Chapter 2, conscious reflection is a natural human activity that can be lost unless it is fostered. In the figure, reflective practice is the main stem from which learning and development can be supported. However, it is not always easy to find the space and time to be reflective, and being reflective also means examining personal values and beliefs which can sometimes be challenging to rationalize. Being reflective can reveal unexpected emotional responses, which can have profound effects at a personal level about understanding the triggers that inhibit or motivate learning. Canning and Callan (2010) argue that it is important for study to build on students' strengths and that it is essential to not only acknowledge past learning experiences but also for students to begin to recognize those aspects of their profession that influence their thinking and practice. These influencing factors are complex and continuously evolving, and it is important to provide the student with the capability to reflect on what is impacting on their practice.

The participants in this research were not only developing their early years practice through their study but had made (whether they realized it or not at the beginning of their study) an emotional investment to their personal learning journey, and in their sense of self and professional identity. To fulfil their commitment to the EYPS programme they needed to engage in reflective practice because, as a professional leading early years practice, their actions had important consequences because they impact on the learning experiences of young children at a critical period of their development.

Greene (1995) suggests that anyone who engages with knowledge sharing through teaching in any type of situation has to think about their own thinking, how they have been influenced and what kind of knowledge they are passing on to others. In the early years, practitioners work closely with other colleagues and collaboration is a way in which shared discussion of personal practice can inform ways of thinking and working, and where values and beliefs can be clarified or can start to form. Canning and Callan (2010, p. 75) suggest that heutagogy involves understanding the impact our learning has had on us and may be realized through 'shared meaning making in a relational, facilitative approach to reflection'. However, to enter into meaningful discussions about practice and supporting children's development, practitioners need to have the confidence to initiate such discussions. Confidence is also needed to voice opinions or to debate with colleagues.

Confidence and motivation

Figure 12.1 illustrates that from the stem of reflective practice, new stems and eventually flowers grow. To cultivate new growth in the form of building knowledge and understanding, to disseminate this others and achieve a personal and professional transition, requires personal motivation and determination to want to engage with new ideas and perspectives and confidence to share learning with others. The participants in the research had already been through several years of study, gaining a foundation degree and usually engaging with continual professional development (CPD) courses. However, engaging with education does not necessarily translate into professional confidence. As Hase and Kenyon point out in Chapter 2, formal education does not necessarily enable what is a natural confidence in our capacity to learn. In fact, it may erode that natural confidence that is inherent, given the right circumstances, in every pre-schooler. Usher et al. (2002) suggest that confidence develops through experience, through being open to new ideas and ways of working, and by not being afraid to try out new ideas. Early years practitioners have opportunities to work with children and their families and are able to use work-based investigation into the experiences of children to support their own professional practice. The EYPS structure enables early years practitioners working in different roles and in different types of settings to reflect on how they see themselves, identify their strengths and areas for development. This approach supports the development of a sense of professional identity and, through engaging in reflection and recognizing accomplishments, confidence is increased. Nicola, a private day nursery room leader for 2- and 3-year-olds commented:

> My confidence has improved because I can see what I do makes a difference to the children. I used to be a bit sceptical of change because I thought it was disruptive to the children, but having talked to other practitioners on the course and listened to what they do, I am much more willing to try new things and the children respond almost immediately so I get instant feedback on my practice. I've found that I have more confidence in taking the child's lead and reading more about children's holistic development has given me confidence to say to the other practitioners in the room, no, it's ok to let them play.

Participation in the EYPS programme has supported early years practitioners becoming active learners and enabling them to trust their learning. Their involvement in developing their knowledge and understanding is linked to their everyday practice which perpetuates learning and reflection. The ability a student develops to reflect upon their experiences of learning and how that experience impacts on their practice with children is important to sustain motivation and to demonstrate the relevance of the EYPS programme to their practice. The connections that students make between learning and practice support a 'spiral of reflection' (Canning and Callan, 2010). The spiral enables confidence and motivation to develop from applying new learning to practice, reflecting on the impact of actions and adapting practice to bring about change. New learning may come from reading about theories or different perspectives on early childhood, a different way of doing something demonstrated at a workshop, discussing with other colleagues, networking with other professionals, making connections through online forums or attending conferences, for example.

The research into the 'spiral of reflection' has concluded that experienced early years practitioners already engage at an intuitive level with reflection and that programmes such as EYPS are significant in supporting practitioners in being consciously reflective. Being consciously reflective means that students are able to recognize emotional triggers in their learning and begin to understand what motivates them and what kind of engagement with learning builds their confidence. Gunnlaugson (2007) suggests that being reflective, but also being critical in examining how an individual approaches learning, can create capacity for change in an individuals' disposition towards learning. It may be that only a small change occurs but, significantly, the student recognizes not only what they have done to make the change, but why the change makes a difference to their learning. Sahera, a pre-school (2–4 years) manager explains:

> When I started my top up degree with EYPS it was because I thought I had to do it. Other practitioners I knew were signing up for it and I didn't want to be left behind. At first it was a chore to study and I started to resent having to give up my free time to do something that I thought I was already qualified in – providing quality childcare. It was about half way through when I realised that this was a chance for me to focus on something I was passionate about – outdoor play. I started to think about studying and learning in a different way – it's hard to explain but I got organised, in my head and in my study. I became more focused, it was like, because I realised I had a real interest in something and could see that in the long run it would make a real difference to my setting and the children, it motivated me and changed the way I approached learning. Doing EYPS has made me understand more about what drives me as a practitioner and to think, 'what do I want out of this and how am I going to get it' – in terms of strategies for learning that work for me.

For Sahera, the motivation that she found from thinking about what she was really interested in (developing her practice), resulted in determination and increased confidence as a learner. She was able to recognize the opportunity to self-direct her interest into focused learning so that she completed the programme, developed her practice, made a difference to the children's experience and developed her knowledge and understanding of something she was passionate about. EYPS is also concerned with developing leadership so the next step concerns influencing others to change their practice.

A shift in thinking

It emerged through the interviews that to influence others, participants needed to reflect on their own level of confidence and motivation and understand their emotional investment and personal learning journey. They also needed to feel secure in their ability to share their knowledge, understanding and ideas. In the flower diagram (Figure 12.1), participants had established a 'stem' of reflective practice and were developing heutagogic strategies to build knowledge and understanding to disseminate to others, and were engaged in the process of articulating personal and professional transitions. The next stage involved the blossoming of 'flowers' where the professional journey and personal empowerment with which participants had engaged, flourished into making a positive difference to children's experiences. Ashton and Newman (2006) suggest that heutagogy situates power in the hands of the learner, because heutagogy supports individuals to self-direct what they do with their knowledge and understanding. The participants made it clear that they did reflect on personal knowledge and understanding and how that might direct personal practice and career decisions. However it was quite a different challenge to shape and influence the thinking of others and realize the potential of 'flowering buds'.

The distance learning aspect in this EYPS programme created a virtual community of practice (Wenger, 1998) where students could engage in formal and informal networking online. The virtual space provided the opportunity for knowledge sharing and confidence building, enhancing students ability to voice their opinions. Claxton (2003) encourages dialogue between practitioners in whatever capacity to promote a never-ending learning journey of both personal and professional qualities. The distance learning supported some students in being able to share practice and opinions in a way that may have been less successful with face-to-face interactions. Dianne, a private day nursery, baby room leader commented:

> I had more confidence when corresponding with other students online. They didn't know me personally and I felt I could say what I thought and they wouldn't judge me on anything else apart from what I talked about. I was more objective because I couldn't physically see them and wasn't worrying about what they thought of me. I think this has helped my confidence in practice, because I have had to lead others for the EYPS, I just think – 'pretend you're that person online'. I have found that the whole process has made me think about what I do and how I influence other practitioners and parents. I wasn't sure if I made a difference before, but doing my degree and the EYPS has made me think I do.

The online interaction with other students has supported transformative learning for Dianne because she has started to think beyond her own learning towards her impact and influence on others. Mezirow (1978) suggests a change in Dianne's frame of reference had taken place, as she started to reflect on the implications of her learning and subsequent practice for other early years practitioners. Realizing the potential impact of the heutagogic strategies that the participants employed through their programme of study supported positive change and a shift in thinking towards practice. Linda, a private day nursery owner reflected:

> It's all the little things that have added up to make the biggest difference. I can't say I have radically changed my practice or been particularly inspiring to my staff, but what has happened is that we talk more. I'm more open to their ideas and more confident to explain what I think and why I think it. I can back up what I say with books that I've read and ideas I have taken on from other people on EYPS. I can justify my position to Ofsted (Office for Standards in Education, England) inspectors and argue why I need to do this or that to my local authority early years advisor . . .

> Some changes I have made here haven't fully worked, but being able to reflect, being empowered to give it a go and know that it will generate discussion and sometimes passionate argument within our team means that I know we are putting the needs of the children first and doing the best for them, which at the end of the day is why I'm in early years in the first place.

Conclusion

The findings from this study suggest that in working towards EYPS early years practitioners have benefited from identifying specific aspects of their practice, how they support others and how these two elements can change and influence practice and improve quality provision for children. Participants recognized the significance of engaging with heutagogic strategies to support their reflective practice and how this has been central to developing confidence and sustaining motivation through a programme of study. Being able to recognize leadership and implementing change has developed through understanding the personal involvement and emotional investment made in the process of learning. For all of the participants in this research project, the personal journey continues so that the outcomes for children or 'flowers' (Figure 12.1) continue to bloom and multiply.

References

Ashton, J. and Elliott, R. (2007), 'Juggling the balls – study, work, family and play: student perspectives on flexible and blended heutagogy', *European Early Childhood Education Research Journal,* 15(2), 167–81.

Ashton, J. and Newman, L. (2006), 'An unfinished symphony: 21st century teacher education using knowledge creating heutagogies', *British Journal of Educational Technology,* 36(6), 825–40.

Canning, N. and Callan, S. (2010), 'Heutagogy: spirals of reflection to empower learners in higher education', *Reflective Practice,* 11(1), 71–82.

Children's Workforce Development Council (CWDC) (2007), *Early Years Professional Status Candidate Handbook.* Leeds: CWDC.

Claxton, G. (2003), *The Intuitive Practitioner: On the Value of Not Always Knowing What One is Doing.* Maidenhead: Open University Press.

Gomm, R. (1993), 'Issues of power in health and welfare', in J. Walmsley, J. Reynolds, P. Shakespeare and R. Wollef (eds), *Health, Welfare and Practice: Reflecting on Roles and Relationships.* California: SAGE, 132–8.

Greene, M. (1995), *Releasing the Imagination: Essay on Education, the Arts and Social Change.* San Francisco, CA: Jossey-Bass.

Gunnlaugson, O. (2007), 'Shedding light on the underlying forms of transformative learning theory: introducing three distinct categories of consciousness', *Journal of Transformative Education,* 5(2), 134–51.

Mezirow, J. (1978), 'Perspective transformation', *Adult Education Quarterly,* 28, 100–10.

Rivera, H. and Tharp, R. (2006), 'A native American community's involvement and empowerment to guide their children's development in the school setting', *Journal of Community Psychology,* 34(4), 435–51.

Tickell, C. (2011), *The Early Years: Foundations for Life, Health and Learning.* London: Crown Copyright.

Usher, R., Bryant, I. and Johnson, R. (2002), 'Self and experience in adult learning', in R. Harrison, F. Reeve, A. Harison and J. Clarke (eds), *Supporting Lifelong Learning: Volume 1, Perspectives on Learning.* London: Routledge and Open University Press, 78–90.

Wenger, E. (1998), *Communities of Practice: Learning, Meaning and Identity.* Cambridge: Cambridge University Press.

13

Transitioning from Pedagogy to Heutagogy

Boon Hou Tay

Summary

Like the improvement of a physical skill, the appreciation of beauty in any form can be developed with practice. This chapter illustrates an important and exciting voyage of discovery through a three-stage learning process in which the learner transitions from pedagogy to heutagogy via andragogy. Apart from stimulating an individual's creative activities, this three-stage learning process enables an individual to make unknowns known.

Introduction

Heutagogy assumes that people: have the potential to learn continuously and in real time by interacting with their environment; learn through their lifespan; can be led to ideas rather than be force fed the wisdom of others; enhance their creativity; and re-learn how to learn (Hase and Tay, 2004). This chapter uses my personal experiences with the Pythagoras Theorem to illustrate an important and exciting voyage of discovery through a three-stage learning process that transits from pedagogy, andragogy, to heutagogy: and with little or no instructor control in the pedagogical and andragogical stages. I am not suggesting that instructor control is irrelevant, instead I am attempting to convey some feeling for a process that, if practiced alone, helps an individual to intuitional glimpses of truth, then a whole realm of discoveries can be achieved through help from mentors, tutors, instructors and supervisors. The essence for this exciting voyage is adapted and refined from that of Huntley (1970, p. 2):

> To induce aesthetic pleasure: select a suitable object or context from the Physical World, acquire the relevant commonsense facts, construct an abstract model for the context, and help yourself to make unknown(s) known.

Aesthetic appreciation – A primer for self-determined learning

My aesthetic appreciation for Pythagoras Theorem was triggered during an outdoor course that I was conducting. I made the following statement to a group (see also Figure 13.1) and the experience was documented in my personal research log (dated 16 November 2005):

> Gentlemen, stand near to the river where you can see a prominent object such as a tree directly across the river; mark the position where you are with a twig; fold a square piece of paper to form a right-angle isosceles triangle; turn to your left and walk in a straight line parallel to the river; count your footsteps along the way; look back along the hypotenuse from time to time until the hypotenuse points directly at the prominent object; record down the total steps as the approximate width of river in metres (of course, the accuracy depends on the length of one's stride) . . . . How fascinating what a piece of paper can do!

This aesthetic appreciation of mine refers to that quality or combinations of qualities that affords keen pleasure to the senses, especially that of sight, or that charms the intellectual or moral faculties (Huntley, 1970). However, only a part of this wide definition concerns us here. We are not interested at the moment in, for example, 'the beauty of holiness' that 'charms' the moral faculties (Huntley, 1970). Our interest lies in the combination of qualities that charm the intellect.

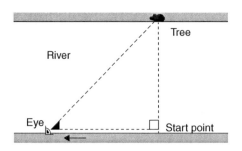

Figure 13.1 Estimating the width of a river.

In Huntley's view, this aesthetic experience, through the interaction between an object (or context) of beauty and an observer, is an emotional rather than a rational mental activity. It consists in the levitation from the unconscious to the surface mind of a memory complex activated by an association mechanism sequential to the visual or aural contemplation of the beautiful object (Allen and Smith, 1999). In other words, emotions are activities of our unconscious minds (Goldblum, 2001). Therefore, the aesthetic experience is the resuscitation of subliminal emotions and beauty is the power to evoke these emotions (Hargreaves and North, 2000).

This leads us to consider the question of whether beauty serves a purpose in the scheme of creation, although beauty appears to serve no utilitarian end. Many of our instincts and associated emotions have been evolved to ensure our bodily survival, but the emotion aroused by a mental image, such as the elegant Pythagoras Theorem, has no such objective. Huntley (1970, p. 20) responded to this objection as follows:

> Man (sic) is by nature a creator. Man is born to create: to fashion beauty, to originate new values. That is his or her supreme vocation. This truth awakens a resonant response deep within us, for we know that one of the most intense joys that the soul of man can experience is that of creativity activity. Ask the artist. Ask the poet. Ask the scientist. Ask the inventor or the neighbour who grows prize roses. They all know the deep spiritual satisfaction associated with the moment of orgasm of creation.

The perspective here is that creativity is a reflection of our Creative Intelligence. Our Creative Intelligence describes how we see and understand the world, our basic beliefs and our personality. Creative Intelligence differs from what is normally considered General Intelligence. General Intelligence, or the Intelligence Quotient (IQ), is characterized as being focused, disciplined, logical, constrained, down-to-earth, realistic, practical, staid, dependable and conservative (Mackintosh, 1998). Creative Intelligence, on the other hand, is expansive, innovative, inventive, unconstrained, daring, uninhabited, fanciful, imaginative, unpredictable, revolutionary and free spirited (Rowe, 2004). Although both types of intelligence rely on how people view and response to the world, creativity focuses on how we think and our strong desire to achieve something new or different.

The notion of creativity leads us to the second natural objection that many would raise: that they had no experience of creative activity. They have added nothing to the store of beauty and their own ideas have been neither new nor original. They have never known the luminous amount of inspiration that widens the bounds of knowledge. They can appreciate, but cannot create beauty.

Huntley (1970, p. 22) provides the answer to this second objection:

> The act of creation and the act of appreciation of beauty are not, in essence, distinguishable. In the moment of appreciation ('I see! Yes, indeed I see! How beautiful!'), the beholder experiences those precise emotions that passed through the mind of the creator in his or her moment of creation.

The above answer illuminates the meaning of empathy ('feeling into') and should be understood by all who seek the aesthetic experience.

If the foregoing arguments are correct, then aesthetic experience serves as a primer for our voyage of discovery. It is the primer that makes us ready to learn. This leads us to the next question: how do we kindle the spark of aesthetic feeling into a flame?

Transitioning through the three stages of learning, namely, pedagogy, andragogy and heutagogy

Pedagogy

Pedagogy is the first stage. As pointed by Huntley (1970), some preliminary education related to the selected object or context is needed. A limited sense of aesthetic appreciation is given; the rest must be acquired. For example, the mathematically uneducated can easily appreciate the two equal sides of a right-angle isosceles triangle: that is given. But the unlimited store of beauty for the three sides of the triangle is reserved for the mathematically trained: it is acquired. This indicates that the path to real aesthetic pleasure is through toil, a principle that holds far beyond the realm of mathematics.

Instead of watching the teacher work in class, we can 're-enact the experiences' that Pythagoras had gone through (Penrose, 2004). Consider the right-angled triangle in Figure 13.2. First, we draw a square from each side of the given right-angled triangle. Second, we cut the square out from each side. Third, we place the largest square on the table. Finally, we cut the smaller square in pieces where necessary and paste the cut-portions onto the largest square.

It is clear that the area of the largest square must be equal to the sum of the areas of the two smaller squares. Besides, it is evident that the edge-length of the large tilted square is the hypotenuse of a right-angled triangle, whose two other sides have lengths equal to the sides of the two smaller squares. We have thus

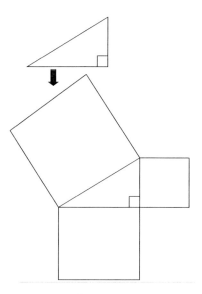

Figure 13.2 A paper-cutting activity for Pythagoras Theorem lesson.

established the Pythagorean theorem: the square on the hypotenuse is equal to the sum of the squares on the other two sides.

Within this stage of learning, it is important to distinguish common sense from refined knowledge (Tay and Hase, 2010). Common sense consists of things we see, hear, smell, and feel. In fact, the paper-cutting exercise for the Pythagoras theorem activity counts as a commonsense fact, as we see that the big square on the hypotheses is indeed a sum of the two smaller squares on the other sides.

According to Pepper (1942), there are three distinguishing features of common sense. First, common sense is not definitely knowable and perceivable. For example, we place an object shaped like a tomato on a table. We can doubt whether it is a tomato and not a cleverly painted piece of wax. Second, common sense is secure. For example, we cannot doubt the fact that something is red and round then and there. Third, common sense is unreliable, irresponsible, and in a word, annoying. See what happens when someone introduces an object, such as a red cherry, that is also red and round: the debate has to be restarted.

In Pepper's view (1942), the indefiniteness of much detail in common sense, its contradictions, its lack of established grounds, drives the mind to seek definiteness, consistency and causes. Thought finds these in criticized refined knowledge, only to discover that these tend to thin out into arbitrary definitions, pointer readings, and tentative hypotheses, propositions or theories.

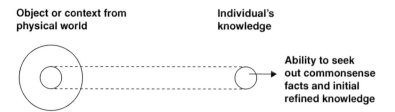

Figure 13.3 Knowledge gained in the pedagogical stage.

However, when responsible cognition does find itself insecure as a result of the very earnestness of its virtue, it has to turn back to common sense, that indefinite and irresponsible source. In other words, refined knowledge exists in a vacuum unless it acknowledges openly the actual, though strange, source of its significance and security in the uncriticized material of common sense. Thus, the circle is completed. Common sense continually demands the responsible criticism of refined knowledge, and refined knowledge sooner or later requires the security of common sense support.

Therefore, it is crucial to seek out as many commonsense facts as possible when in the pedagogical stage. Figure 13.3 summarizes a person's knowledge with respect to the object or context from the physical world in pedagogy.

A previous paper (Tay and Hase, 2004) described how doctoral students went through the three phases of pedagogy, andragogy and heutagogy in their candidature. Most of the students had technical, engineering or science backgrounds yet were undertaking social science research on their organizations using action research. They were completely unfamiliar with social science as a discipline and with action research as a methodology. So, initially the students were very reliant on their supervising team and asked many questions as they tried to make sense of what they were being exposed to. Referring to Figure 13.3, the students were seeking out commonsense facts and initial refined knowledge.

Andragogy

Andragogy, adult learning (Knowles, 1970) is the second stage. The primary emphasis of this stage is to construct an abstract representation for a phenomenon (Tay and Hase, 2004). This stage provides us with the opportunity to acquire more insight into our problem situation, and seek refined knowledge through the process of articulating, structuring and critically evaluating a model of what we are experiencing. Modelling is purposive (Ford and Bradshaw, 1993) and it determines what should be modelled, how to model it and what can be ignored.

This is in accord with the notion of andragogy. According to Giunchiglia and Walsh (1992, p. 329), modelling is:

- The process of mapping a representation of a problem called the 'ground' representation, onto a new representation, called the 'abstract' representation, which:
  - helps deal with the problem in the original space by preserving certain desirable properties and
  - is simpler to handle as it is constructed from the ground representation by 'throwing away details'.

The term 'approximation', that can be inferred from the second statement above, does not mean a reduced and simpler model but a generalized model (Gaines, 1993) that includes all our mental associations with certain physical structures (the desirable properties) in the physical word. The term 'simplification' refers to the removal of undesirable properties not related to our aesthetic appreciation such as our other mentality associated with the multifarious irritations, pleasures, worries, excitements and the like that fill our daily lives.

The importance of abstract representation can be appreciated via Mendeleev's great achievement in deriving the Periodic Table used in chemistry. Mendeleev (1834–1907) was the first to have the courage to leave open gaps in the classification instead of trying to impose an artificial completeness on it. This matters because in the 1860s only about 60 elements had been discovered. The holes in Mendeleev's table were like daring predictions that yet undiscovered entities must exist. The holes in Mendeleev's table imply the application of boundary that is not imposed from outside the system, rather it emerges because of differences within the system itself (Eoyang 1996).

We can use the boundaries of a known-system to 'enclose' the area of 'unknown' (see Figure 13.4). The deliberate open gap in Mendeleev's table has contributed in the following ways (DeLande, 2004): Medeleev predicted the existence of germanium on the basis of a gap near silicon; Curie later predicted the existence of radium on the basis of its neighbour, barium; a hundred years later, the set of transition elements helped the medical communities to introduce chemotherapy for treating cancers. Chemotherapy is definitely something of which Medeleev himself was not aware in his time. Therefore, Medeleev created an abstract representation that has a focus for the future.

The paper-cutting activity for Pythagoras Theorem does give us some 'reasons' for believing that the theorem has to be true. However, for model construction,

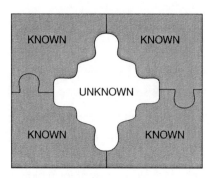

Figure 13.4 The known and the unknown.

we require formal argument given by a succession of logical steps. For example, 'Is a square something that is geometrically possible?'

In building up the notion of geometry, we re-enact the experiences of Euclid (325 BC–265 BC). Euclid's first postulate asserts that there is a (unique) straight-line segment connecting any two points. His second postulate asserts the unlimited (continuous) extensibility of any straight-line segment. His third postulate asserts the existence of a circle with any centre and with any value for its radius. His fourth postulate asserts the equality of all right angles. His fifth postulate is a parallel postulate: it turns out that the fifth postulate is what we need to establish the notion of a square.

The fifth postulate asserts that if two straight-line segments 'a' and 'b' in a plane both intersect another straight line 'c' (the traversal of 'a' and 'b') such that the sum of the interior angles on the same side of 'c' is less than two right angles, then 'a' and 'b' will intersect somewhere. If a transversal to a pair of straight lines meets so that the sum of the interior angles one side of the transversal is two right angles, then the lines of the pair are indeed parallel. Moreover, it immediately follows that any other transversal of the pair has just the same angle property. Keeping the right angles and the lines parallel, shift any two adjacent lines until all the lines are of equal length. This is basically just what we needed for the construction of squares.

Figure 13.5 provides a diagrammatic representation of how the learner makes sense of the world by bringing into play previous experience or knowledge, which is the essence of andragogy.

Using the previous example of candidates undergoing a PhD programme, Tay and Hase (2004) found that after the initial pedagogical stage learners started to bring their own experience to the research. Thus, they started to become

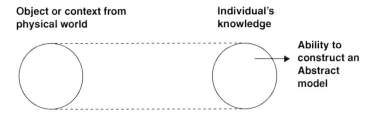

Figure 13.5 Knowledge gained in the andragogical stage.

less dependent on the teachers and new information, and more focused on integrating their new learning with their previous experience. This is the essence of andragogy and a shift of emphasis from the teacher to the learner.

Heutagogy

The last stage in our learning process involves higher levels of autonomy which Hase and Kenyon (2000) call self-determined learning or heutagogy. People enter this stage to seek out new knowledge associated with the 'deliberate open gaps' in the abstract model. This seeking action is known as generalizing (Tay and Hase 2010) and it is central to the definition and creation of valid public knowledge.

However, Carel and Gamez (2004) raise an issue on the restrictions posed by boundaries. Limits only make sense if we know what lies on either side of them. If our knowledge is limited in some way, we will be unable to know what lies beyond its limit and so any attempt to describe this limit and make it convincing will have to implicitly or explicitly transgress this limit in order to identify it as a limit. In other words, the attempt to set a limit to a piece of knowledge ends up including, within that piece of knowledge, what it is trying to put out of bounds.

Lawson (2004) pointed out that this restriction is caused by our notion of 'the world'. It makes it look as if the world is already differentiated, awaiting the descriptions of language: as if diligent scientists could uncover the ultimate building blocks of matter and we would know of what the world is made. Instead, Lawson (2004) proposed that we hold the world as 'open' (our doing, being and experiencing within the world). It is we who make sense of it through 'closure' (our critical reflection). We, who through the process of closure, hold openness as a complex array of things. Closure can be conceived, therefore, as a process that enables the flux of openness to be held as differentiated bits. Closure is the process of realizing identities, or realizing things. It is the mechanism by which we hold that which is different as one and the same. All of our sensations, all of our perceptions, all of our descriptions of the world are the products of closure. They are not open, nor do they have anything in common with openness. Language is one form of closure where words and sentences do not refer to the world. Instead they offer a way of holding openness as something and, by doing so, they enable us to intervene.

For example, there is no right-angle triangle pattern in the river. Once we have seen the right-angle triangle pattern, we can use it to estimate the width of the river. Therefore, closure does not need to have something in common with openness in order to enable intervention, and this means that no closure or set of closures is going to cut through to openness, and is going to be able to describe how things are in openness. Closure itself is an attempt to say the unsayable. In Lawson's view, closures do not get closer to reality as we refine them. We do not gradually approach a true description – as we often suppose of science – and the more we do so the more the failure of the closures begins to show. These failures do not tell us how the world is, but the manner of their failure tells us something about what the world is not, and they are powerful as they are capable of changing how we think and what we can achieve. This notion is central to heutagogy in describing the way in which people make sense of the world in their own time, when the connections are made and not at some predetermined moment (Hase and Kenyon, Chapter 2).

Let us try to address a 'deliberate open gap' in the Pythagoras Theorem, also known as the Pythagorean Catastrophe (Penrose 2004). Can one find a rational number (i.e. a fraction) whose square is precisely the number 2? This comes from the Pythagorean Theorem itself as we can have a square whose side length is unity, then its diagonal length is a number whose square $1^2 + 1^2 = 2$, where $a^2 = 1^2$, $b^2 = 1^2$, and $c^2 = 2$. It is catastrophic for Pythagoreans as they are only aware of whole numbers. Let us see why the equation $c^2 = 2$ has no solution for the positive integer c. Simply use a scientific calculator to determine the value for $\sqrt{2}$. It turns out that $\sqrt{2} = 1.4142135623730950488016887 2 \ldots$ and this clearly demonstrates that 2 does not have a whole number square root. In fact, the manner of this failure tells mathematicians something about what the Pythagoras Theorem is not and leads mathematicians ultimately to the real number system. Figure 13.6 shows the new knowledge acquired at the end of this stage.

The doctoral students referred to earlier shifted to the natural learning state of heutagogy when they were able to experiment, fail, discover and then know in their own terms, undirected and unrestrained. Learning became self-determined.

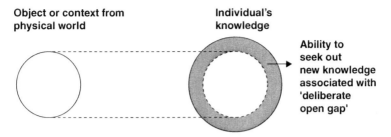

Figure 13.6 Knowledge gained in the heutagogical stage.

Conclusion

The undoubted role of beauty for the underlying workings of the physical world, and aesthetic criteria are fundamental to the development of refined knowledge for their own sake, thereby providing both the drives towards discovery and a powerful guide to truth. The thrust that underscores the three-stage learning process is our desire to go beyond the simple acquisition of skills and knowledge as a learning process. The process emphasizes a holistic development in the learner of an independent capability, the capacity for questioning one's values and assumptions and the critical role of the system–environment interface (Hase and Tay 2004). Therefore, the three-stage learning process is a process that enables us to make unknowns known. It is an activity about activity. It has not ended – has hardly in fact begun, although the publication of a piece of refined knowledge such as this chapter may suggest it as complete. But the infinitude of openness stands not for the closing of a ring; it is rather a gateway. Always beckoning, approached but never achieved: perhaps this is the authentic life experience that we desire, that is, doing, being and experiencing within the world.

References

Allen, R. and Smith, M. (1999), *Film Theory and Philosophy*. Oxford: Oxford University Press.

Carel, H. and Gamez, D (2004), *What Philosophy Is*. London: Continuum.

Eoyang, G. H. (1996), *A Brief Introduction to Complexity in Organisations*. Retrieved 23 August 2012 from: www.winternet.com/~eoyang/.

Ford, K. M. and Bradshaw, J. M. (1993), 'Introduction: knowledge acquisition as modeling', *International Journal of Intelligent Systems*, 8, 1–7.

Gaines, B. R. (1993), 'Modeling practical reasoning', *International Journal of Intelligent Systems*, 8, 51–70.

Giunchiglia, F. and Walsh, T. (1992), 'A theory of abstraction', *Artificial Intelligence*, 57, 323–89.

Goldblum, N. (2001), *The Brain-Shaped Mind: What the Brain Can Tell us about the Mind*. Cambridge: Cambridge University Press.

Hargreaves, D. J. and North, A. C. (2000), *The Social Psychology of Music*. Oxford: Oxford University Press.

Hase, S. and Kenyon, C. (2000), 'From andragogy to heutagogy', *Ultibase*, December. Retrieved 28 November 2012 from: http://ultibase.rmit.edu.au/Articles/dec00/hase2. htm.

Hase, S. and Tay, B. H. (2004), 'Capability for complex systems: beyond competence', *Proceedings, Systems Engineering/ Test and Evaluation Conference*, Adelaide, April.

Huntley, H. (1970), *The Divine Proportion: A Study in Mathematical Beauty*. New York: Dover Publications.

Knowles, M. (1970), *The Modern Practice of Adult Education: Andragogy versus Pedagogy*. New York: Associated Press.

Lawson, H. (2004), 'Philosophy as saying the unsayable', in H. Carel and D. Gamez (eds), *What Philosophy Is*. London: Continuum, 283–90.

Mackintosh, N. J. (1998), *IQ and Human Intelligence*. Oxford: Oxford University Press.

Penrose, R. (2004), *The Road to Reality. A Complete Guide to the Laws of the Universe*. New York: Alfred A. Knopf.

Rowe, A. J. (2004), *Creative Intelligence: Discovering the Innovative Potential in Ourselves and Others*. New Jersey: Pearson Education, Inc.

Tay, B. H. and Hase, S. (2004), 'The role of action research in workplace PhDs', *Research in Action Learning and Action Research Journal*, 9(1), 81–92.

—. (2010), 'Lemmas for action research', *Action Research Action Learning (ALAR)*, 16(2), 3–33.

14

Innovations in Community Education

Roslyn Foskey

Summary

Aligning the concept of adult learning with heutagogy provides important insights on the reflexivity that occurs when interactive theatre is used in a community learning project. The Mature Men Matter project aimed to promote the health and well-being of older rural Australian men, through encouraging peer support. The theatre process allowed audience members, in conversation with the actors (remaining in character), to shift, change, contextualize and expand upon a research-based scenario. This process allowed those taking part – both actors-in-character and audience members – to consider the situation presented through a spiralling process incorporating both reflection-in-action and reflection-on-action.

Introduction

The project discussed in this chapter, Mature Men Matter, was centred on an interactive theatre process undertaken between 2002 and 2007 in rural towns and villages in the north of New South Wales, Australia. The idea to take the Mature Men Matter performances out to rural communities came from participants who had experienced the process in a workshop for older male community volunteers held at the University of New England in 2002. Participation in the community performances was voluntary and the audiences were comprised mainly of older rural men. The audiences also included retired working-class men who are often identified by adult educators and health professionals as hard to engage in learning. In several of the performances, some of the men's partners also attended, along with health, aged care and community workers (Foskey 2007). More than 30 performances were given, with audience numbers usually between 15 and 30, though around 200 people attended a performance given at a national farming conference.

This chapter explores the Mature Men Matter experience through the concept of heutagogy, which incorporates an ontology, or way of being, applicable to the ever-changing circumstances of life in rural Australia. The originators of the approach have described heutagogy as a 'child of complexity theory', with learning being self-determined by the learner within adaptive systems, which are unpredictable, open and non-linear (Hase and Kenyon, 2007, p. 111). Within heutagogy the experience of learning is therefore, understood to be 'emergent, self-organised, adaptive and dynamic' (Hase, 2004, p.2). This is an apt description of the interactive theatre process as it moved from the scripted scenes to become an improvised performance.

In bringing people together through interactive theatre, the Mature Men Matter project became an epistemology of learning through active engagement with the growing complexity of life (Nicolaides and Yorks, 2008). This creative process was focused on promoting the well-being of older men. Well-being encompasses the proactive engagement in living and involves opportunities for the 'expression of a broad range of human potentialities: intellectual, social, emotional and physical' (Ryff and Singer, 1998, p. 2).

An interactive process

At the core of the theatre-based learning process used within Mature Men Matter was the opportunity for the audience to engage with the characters, and thereby to explore the dilemma incorporated in the initial scripted scenarios. The scenarios were developed by the author in collaboration with theatre professional Grant Dodwell, who wrote the scripted scenarios. Grant was also the director and performed one of the characters. The scenario usually featured three characters. Each of the actors had a background as an adult educator, as well as having performed in community and professional theatre. The actors were age-appropriate to their role and were experienced in improvisation. To assist them with performing and improvising their roles, the actors were provided with detailed background notes on the characters.

The scenarios used in Mature Men Matter were based on research and consultations undertaken by the author over a number of years, but were not a verbatim reproduction of interview data. Rather, the scenarios blended together ideas and insights from a variety of research and consultation processes undertaken in regional Australia to create a story instantly recognizable to the audience, yet fictional. In this way, along with being the catalyst for action learning, the scenario also became another cycle of collaborative action research. Here is one of the scenarios:

> Jack is a widowed farmer aged in his 70s living on a farm about twenty kilometres from town. Jack has some health problems that are a concern to his daughter. It is becoming difficult for Jack to manage the day-to-day demands of both the farm business and running the house. His daughter Julia (a divorcee who works at the local school) and her new partner, Adrian (a local schoolteacher who recently moved to town from the city) come for a visit on Sunday afternoon. They express their concern about the condition of the farm and the house, and put pressure on Jack to consider a move into town. Similar conversations have obviously occurred on previous visits. This conversation ends in an impasse and this is Jack's dilemma.

Following the performance of the scripted scenario the audience were invited to engage in a discussion with the characters (with the actors improvising their responses in character). Through this facilitated interchange the audience were engaged in a reflexive process as they bent back upon their own experiences in shaping the story in collaboration with the characters. At the same time both the audience and actors in character, were engaged in reflection-in-action through facilitated interchange to explore the emotional and experiential dimensions of the scenario. In doing so, they were engaging in a form of serious play (Palus and Horth, 2005), reflecting on their own experiences, values and assumptions, as well as on those of their characters.

Once the scenario had been teased out in some detail, the facilitator invited the audience to select and coach one character. The character chosen depended upon the emergent dynamics. The audience made suggestions to their character to shift the situation beyond the impasse reached in the scripted scenes. Audience members then observed their suggestions being applied to the situation in an improvised replay of the initial scenes by the coached character, along with the responses of the other characters to these shifts. This was followed by another dialogic process, an opportunity for both the characters and audience members to reflect on the action in the replay. Finally the actors de-roled explaining how their life experiences may be similar or different to the character they had portrayed. In most workshops this performance process lasted around 90 minutes and was undertaken without any formal break between sections.

The learning process in incorporating interactive theatre in a heutagogical approach can be understood as involving spirals of action and reflection. Engagement with the issues that emerge through this process extends beyond the performance event, in both organized and informal ways. In this chapter the focus is on examining the qualities and dynamics of learning introduced through the interactive theatre process, rather than on the follow-on elements.

Creating the space for participation

One metaphor for theatrical performance is as a flow-through container, as 'a porous, flexible gatherer' (Schechner, 1995, p. 41). The performance of a story can be seen as a public act, a communal experiencing, actively involving a group comprised of the tellers along with the audience for the telling (King, 2003). However, when stories are shared in a conventional theatre environment they easily become caught up within the form of aesthetics that produced the modern, spatially private self and the modern spatiality of knowledge construction (Berg and Longhurst, 2003; Crang and Thrift, 2000; Frost and Yarrow, 1990). Taking the performance into non-theatre venues is therefore necessary to provide the opportunities for an interchange of ideas and experiences that provide learning for both actors and audience alike.

Conventional theatre venues impose a duality between self and other, observed and observer, fixed through an architectural form based around the separation of the spectacle [performance] and receptacle [audience] (Crang and Thrift, 2000; Merrifield, 2000). The public/private duality underlying the separation of stage and audience in conventional theatre has also served to 'reinforce dominant notions of femininity and masculinity' (Whitehead, 2002, p. 114). In conventional theatre through darkening the auditorium during the performance the audience are being protected from public view as they observe, assess and emotionally react to the portrayal of other lives.

It is through this commoditization of space that the possible range of performances is contained. Due to this inherent inflexibility of conventional theatre spaces, non-theatre venues were, in the main, selected for the Mature Men Matter performances. One of the actors who has an academic background in Theatre Studies, described these performance spaces as having more in common with Medieval theatre with its improvised performance spaces, than with Modern theatre (pers. com., 9 December 2006).

Applied Theatre is a term used for such participatory forms, in particular for those forms of Community Theatre that occur outside traditional venues. The term Applied Theatre was coined for 'activities which use the skills and techniques of theatre for functions not usually associated with theatre' (Millett, 2003, p. 2). A characteristic of Applied Theatre is its liminality, in the sense of a space opened and a place created between the folds of everyday life. As Schechner (1988) noted, non-conventional theatre exists in the creases of Western society, in areas of instability and disturbance, yet these are also the areas with the potential to bring changes to the social topography.

In selecting the non-theatre venues for the performances the quest was for a readily accessible, yet neutral venue, which could be shaped to create an intimate learning environment. At times, despite the best of intentions, as community outsiders we got the venue choice wrong. Sometimes this was because of the community dynamics, or poor advice from our local collaborators; at other times because of issues like unanticipated noise levels in the room, from adjoining rooms or outside which impeded participation. It is hard to be a self-determined learner when you cannot hear what is being said!

It was also vital to consider the group dynamics. In critiquing some uses of Applied Theatre within corporate, workplace and institutional settings, Ackroyd (2001, p. 5), emphasized the importance of allowing for dissent and non-compliance among the participants. This is crucial because, no matter what the performance setting is, Applied Theatre is never neutral, there are always power relationships involved (Nissley et al., 2004). In Mature Men Matter the goal was to create an open environment, one in which there was respect for differing perspectives. In the process, audience members were invited, but never required, to participate in the facilitated dialogue with the characters.

In the physical setting for the Mature Men Matter performances there were no curtains to separate the stage area from the audience. The stage area was not raised above the audience, and the performance occurred in full light. The actors did not use any special costumes, nor wear stage make-up, and any props were basic and mostly found on site or borrowed on the day.

Wherever possible the seating in the venue was arranged to form a semi-circle around the imaginary stage area. There were no sets and no special lighting was used, although in one notable case the 'stage' area was so dull once darkness fell it would have been difficult to see the actors on the improvised stage. On that occasion floodlights were borrowed at the last moment from the local State Emergency Service Group.

The imaginary wall separating the stage area and the audience was broken following the scripted scenarios, bringing the audience members directly into a dialogue with the characters. This helped to eliminate the compartmentalized relationship between actors and audience that is found in conventional theatre, and between expert and lay person as typically occurs in health education workshops. Here the health experts were required to embrace collaborative processes beyond their control. However, this letting go of control to allow for the emergence of capability-enhancing relationships was not always easy. In arts–health partnerships there is the potential for theatre to become a space for resistance, insubordination and escape from gender, class and age-related stereotypes. But this escape may be threatened by the dominance of biomedical knowledge. As Hase and Kenyon (2007) noted, the acquisition of expert-determined knowledge should not be confused with true learning.

Learning through theatre

So how is learning to be understood in the context of an interactive theatre process centred on the lives of older rural Australian men? Learning conceptualized through the lens of complexity theory, extends beyond an individual's capacity to perform competently and to apply knowledge in predictable circumstances, rather learning can be seen as the extension and application of their capabilities in novel circumstances (Hase and Kenyon 2007). This conceptualization overlaps with the qualities that the Mature Men Matter project sought to achieve through using theatre to make the familiar strange. This change occurred through exposing the audience to different perspectives on issues associated with everyday human relationships within a rural Australian context.

In order to create an environment for individual and social learning, the performances themselves needed to provide more than the passivity of experiential relief for the audience members (Gesser-Edelsburg et al., 2006; Schutzman and Cohen-Cruz 1999). The most powerful forms of Applied Theatre use theatrical models that encourage audience members to find themselves, and their voices, in and through the performance process (Nissley et al., 2004). The interactive theatre process provided a novel and creative situation because it was based within the life experiences of the participants. It also featured characters that were based on archetypes who were open to change (in contrast to the stereotypes which can often characterize professional discourse).

A range of research has identified important differences in the ways those employed in the health system, and ordinary community members understand and describe health and ageing (Carel, 2008; Frank, 2000; Mol, 2006). The everyday practices of health and care professionals are typically based on the divide between expert and lay person, in which the expert's role is to recognize the problem, make a correct diagnosis and recommend the most effective treatment. At performances there were always some health professionals in attendance, not only to participate in the experience, but also to provide any advice or support immediately after the performance should that become necessary. During performances, the health and aged care workers tended to draw on their professional knowledge and practices to diagnose the older character in the scenario as having health problems and being in need of their services. There was an assumption that the outcomes for the older male character could be 'foretold and pre-scripted' through applying expert knowledge to the situation (Taylor, 1998, p. 83).

How this situation (of assumed ill health) was handled depended upon the quality of the facilitation, which was a difficult process to get just right; as Hase (2011) has pointed out, transformative learning processes tend to occur at the edge of chaos. In one setting the facilitator assumed that to be open meant being laissez faire, which allowed the professionals in the audience to effectively disempower the other members of the audience by dominating the discussions. However, too much control of the interaction was also inappropriate, as this silenced the differences in perspective among the audience – it dulled the edge of the chaos dynamic so important in the learning process. It was when facilitation was undertaken with a light touch, yet focused on enabling equitable participation, that the professionals in the audience did not dominate the interactions. The actors also assisted in this process by subverting didactic suggestions through humour. In this environment other members of the audience were able to connect more reflectively and imaginatively with all the characters. This allowed several interpretations to emerge, helping to subvert prescriptive one-dimensional understandings of the dilemma in the scenario. This freedom to have a range of options allowed the creation of shared meaning in ways which often extended beyond language to embodied interaction, including gestures such as leaning forward, unfolding of arms, shared laughter or a roll of the eyes.

The theatre experience

Through the interactive process the audience in Mature Men Matter were brought into dialogue with the characters during the performance, where they were able to change the initial scripted scenario. The shift in engagement was captured in the following descriptions from participants:

> **Farmer:** The power of this process is that it tackles the problem indirectly, as Adrian [a character] should have been doing. . . . The process you fellows have used today, shows that if you approach it from an indirect way, it's not upfront, people are looking at a third person relationship with the issue.

> **Retired Farm Worker:** Yeh, it sort of makes you put someone else's shoes on and you think, gee yeh, now how would I react? If someone tried to tell me to do something, or make me to do something, I would be like that. I would act and I would not do it. But I think with the right persuasion it would come about. When you get to the first part of the scenario, and then the second part, when they come back in and they sit down and it's all revamped [i.e. the improvised replay of the initial scene]. From the input of the public that was there, the people that attended it, it really is amazing how it confirms how a man would think differently.

Even though these two men in the audience came from the same community, and both had backgrounds in farming, it is noticeable how differently they articulated their experience of the performance. This difference in their describing of their engagement in the event, dependent on social position, was an important emergent theme within the research on the Mature Men Matter experience.

In the extract below the theatre process is described from an actor's perspective explaining the multiple dimensions involved and the move from entertainment to serious play.

> I always felt that it started off and that I was the entertainment: as the actors, we were the entertainment. It was almost fun playing that to a certain degree, we would go in and set up and it would be a very familiar place for the audience, like ·a Bowling Club and all those things and they were going to be entertained. They were very pleased that we were there to entertain them, but afterwards there was always a shift, quite a fundamental shift, and I think that came through. Certainly in my case it came through that whole work of allowing myself to be vulnerable, not only in the playing of the scenario, but also in the improvisation and that in-between part. For me the really important part was when they were questioning us in role.

Mature Men Matter workshops provided an environment in which audience members were able to reflect on their own experiences and thereby generate ideas and suggestions within the context of the scenario. In this process those older men, who may previously have been left voiceless and invisible in expert-led community health information and education events, were often able to contribute their insights, skills and knowledge. The impact of this experience on the participants was described by one of the actors, in this way:

> Repeatedly on our tours men would come up and say (something like): 'I know just how you feel Jack' (Continuing to identify me with my character in the play!) 'I (or my father, my aunt, my nephew) faced exactly the same dilemma'. They would then tell me how the problem was, or was not, solved and how they felt about it. Sometimes they became quite emotional in the telling. Similar discussions went on among participants. It seemed to me that these men were eager to unburden themselves and that they were willing to do so after identifying with the characters in the play.

This process provided a unique context in which to explore the similarities and differences in the ways members of the audience positioned the characters within the theatre process. It also challenged common presumptions of older Australian men's emotional and communication deficiencies, and health and community care workers communication proficiencies. That is, it helped to highlight the superficiality of the sympathetic approach which can characterize professional dialogue, particularly where it is centred on normative stereotypes. As Jack memorably responded in the improvised replay on one occasion as his daughter applied the suggestions provided by a group of nurses: 'So this is what you call the soft touch is it?' This can be contrasted with the empathic engagement of the audience in other performances, in ways which then shaped the replay and fundamentally shifted the relational dynamics.

Learning through serious play

Serious play is akin to child play, rather than childish and diversionary entertainment (Palus and Horth, 2005). Interactive theatre can provide a safe environment for playful learning on the edge of chaos, allowing the complexities and subtleties of an issue or problem to emerge. Through the qualities that interactive theatre creates there is the potential for a healthy form of disorder that can expose and undermine habituated patterns of social discourse.

Improvisation, which was at the core of this playful process, is spontaneous action. In improvising, actors focused on the moment and context, yet also drew on their own experiences (Crossan, 1998). Although improvisation introduces an unscripted element in performance, it also involves audience members in a collaborative and reflective process which combines accessing the past in enhancing and enriching action in the experience of the present (Crossan et al., 2005). It is this folding of past into the present which introduces a powerful sense of movement.

It was the interaction between audience and characters which allowed the emergence of a learning environment 'simultaneously generated from all points of awareness' bending back upon the point of perception in ways which challenged 'linear, time-space oriented thought' (Linds, 2005, p. 110).

The process also opened up the possibility of breaking common assumptions that tend to treat identity as static and additive, link masculinity to pathology, ageing to dependency and passivity and to regard rurality as peripheral (Angus and Reeve, 2006; Griffiths, 2002; Macdonald, 2005; Peterson, 1998). There was an opportunity to play with the boundaries of what is, and what is not, permissible in discussing later life challenges. In the Mature Men Matter performances there emerged the opportunity for different ways of discussing older male emotionality.

For example, in one performance the audience chose the oldest character, Mick, to coach, thereby empowering him within the context of his relationships as in this extract:

Man 1 (aged in his 90s): Is there anything you, you really like doing?

Mick (played by an actor aged in late 70s): Well, I don't know, I mean, I used to fish a lot and I can't really explain to you why I couldn't care less now. My old creel and all that is down in the shed gathering dust. One of these days . . .

Man 1: I was really asking, really asking if there is anything you like doing that helps other people, because that's where you give and you lose yourself, in what you're giving.

Man 2 (aged in his 70s): Yes.

Mick: That's a pretty good point.

Man 2: Yep, and why don't you do it for the other two? You can do this for the other two because you know them, you're the catalyst, you're the common factor to the other two. You could help them see themselves and perhaps change, and by doing so you might change yourself, and give yourself, as he said, an interest. How 'bout that?

What is interesting here is the recommendation to the character of a shift in perspective within the coaching process. Interactive theatre created the opportunity for those actively involved as actors and audience members to bend back upon their lives, actively engaging in the negotiation of meaning. This introduced the potential for those involved as actors and audience members to subvert the master narratives of deficiency and pathology associated with ageing. The mature men seized the opportunity to assert their ideas in a way that reshaped the oldest character as an active agent of positive change, rather than as a passive recipient of services. In doing so, they were not only creating their own meaning, but also promoting a communal sense of well-being.

Conclusion

Mature Men Matter was not simply the re-presentation of previous research as a performance. In each performance the imaginary wall that normally divides the stage from the audience was broken. Through this process there was the potential for the scenario, which was relevant to the life experiences of the participants, to become the catalyst for a form of communal experimentation, involving both actors and audience, through which models and metaphors for life could be explored, tried out and reviewed.

The interactive theatre process used as a medium for learning demonstrated the capability of many of the older members of the audience in playing with, and undermining, class, ageist and gendered stereotypes. It most certainly challenged the idea that older males are difficult to engage in learning around difficult issues. On the contrary, the Mature Men Matter project demonstrated the value of providing a more meaningful context for learning engagement. The process also highlighted the importance of paying attention to the relational dynamics within the group if we are to enable the shift from expert-determined to self-determined learning envisaged in heutagogy.

The Mature Men Matter project illustrates the benefits of adopting a creative learner-determined process of engagement. It also highlights the importance of the learning environment. These environments are so often shaped through public/private, lay/professional, gender, class and age-based divides. These divisions are not only embedded within Western educational practices, but are also in the buildings in which such practices tend to occur. Learning on the edge of chaos takes us into liminal learning environments that allow for new patterns of understanding to emerge, but in which there is also the risk of disappearing into oblivion.

References

Ackroyd, J. (2001), 'Applied theatre: problems and possibilities', *Applied Theatre Researcher*, 1. Retrieved 3 August 2005 from: www.gi.edu.au/centre/cpci/atr/journal/article1_number1.htm.

Angus, J. and Reeve, P. (2006), 'Ageism: a threat to "ageing well" in the 21st century', *The Journal of Applied Gerontology*, 25(2), 137–52.

Berg, L. and Longhurst, R. (2003), 'Placing masculinities and geography', *Gender, Place and Culture*, 10(4), 351–60.

Carel, H. (2008), *Illness: The Cry of the Flesh*. Stocksfield: Acumen.

Crang, M. and Thrift, N. (2000), 'Introduction', in M. Crang and N. Thrift (eds), *Thinking Space*. London: Routledge, 1–30.

Crossan, M. (1998), 'Improvisation in action', *Organization Science*, 9(5), 593–9.

Crossan, M., Cuhna, M., Vera, D. and Cuhna, J. (2005), 'Time and organizational improvisation', *Academy of Management Review*, 30(1), 129–45.

Foskey, R. (2007), 'Mature men matter: interactive theatre in a learning project enhancing the wellbeing of older rural Australian men', PhD thesis submitted to the University of New England, 5 August.

Frank, A. (2000), 'The standpoint of storyteller', *Qualitative Health Research*, 10(3), 354–65.

Frost, A. and Yarrow, R. (1990), *Improvisation in Drama*. London: Macmillan.

Gesser-Edelsburg, A., Guttman, N. and Israelashvili, M. (2006), 'Educational drama and the dilemma of "false catharsis": lessons for theory and practice from a study of anti-drug plays in Israel', *Research in Drama Education*, 11(3), 293–311.

Griffiths, T. (2002), 'The outside country', in T. Bonyhady and T. Griffiths (eds), *Words for Country: Landscape and Language in Australia*. Sydney: UNSW Press, 222–44.

Hase, S. (2004), 'Heutagogy and developing capable people and capable workplaces: strategies for dealing with complexity'. Paper presented at the *Workplace Learning Conference*, Alberta, May. Retrieved 7 December 2012 from: www.win.ualberta.ca/papers/pdf/17.pdf.

—. (2011), 'Learner defined curriculum: heutagogy and action learning in vocational training', *Journal of Applied Research*, Special Edition on Action Research. Retrieved 20 January 2012 from: www.sitjar.sit.ac.nz.

Hase, S. and Kenyon, C. (2007), 'Heutagogy: a child of complexity theory', *Complicity: An International Journal of Complexity and Education*, 4(1), 111–18.

King, T. (2003), *The Truth about Stories*. Toronto: Anansi.

Linds, W. (2005), 'Drama facilitation: twisting and turning in "strange loops"', *Proceedings of the 2005 Complexity Science and Educational Research Conference*, 20–22 November, Loranger, Louisiana, 107–13. Retrieved 1 July 2006 from: www.complexityandeducation.ca.

Macdonald, J. (2005), *Environments for Health*. London: Earthscan.

Merrifield, A. (2000), 'Henri Lebrevre: a socialist in space', in M. Crang and N. Thrift (eds), *Thinking Space*. London: Routledge, 314–47.

Millett, J. (2003), 'Applied theatre taught and caught', *Applied Theatre Researcher*, 4(8), 1–9. Retrieved 20 March 2012 from: www.griffith.edu.au/centre/cpci/atr/.

Mol, A. (2006), 'Cutting surgeons, walking patients: some complexities involved in comparing', in J. Law and A. Mol (eds), *Complexities Social Studies of Knowledge Practices*. Durham: Duke University Press, 218–57.

Nicolaides, A. and Yorks, L. (2008), 'An epistemology of learning through', *Emergence: Complexity and Organization*, 10(1), 50–61.

Nissley, N., Taylor, S. and Houden, L. (2004), 'The politics of performance in organizational theatre-based training and interventions', *Organization Studies*, 25(5), 817–39.

Palus, C. J. and Horth, D. M. (2005), 'Leading creatively: the art of making sense', *Ivey Business Journal*, September/October, 1–8.

Peterson, A. (1998), *Unmasking the Masculine: 'Men' and 'Identity' in a Sceptical Age*. London: Sage Publications.

Ryff, C. and Singer, B. (1998), 'The contours of positive human health', *Psychological Inquiry*, 9(1), 1–28.

Schechner, R. (1988), *Performance Theory: Revised and Expanded Edition*. New York: Routledge.

—. (1995), *The Future of Ritual*. London: Routledge,

Schutzman, M. and Cohen-Cruz, J. (1999) (eds), *Playing Boal: Theatre, Therapy, Activism*. London: Routledge.

Taylor, P. (1998), 'Beyond the systematic and rigorous', in J. Saxton and C. Miller (eds), *The Research of Practice: The Practice of Research*. British Columbia, Victoria: IDEA Publications, 71–88.

Whitehead, S. (2002), *Men and Masculinities: Key Themes and New Directions*. Cambridge: Polity.

15

Where to Next?

Stewart Hase and Chris Kenyon

Summary

This chapter doesn't attempt to foresee the future too far: life is too complex and unpredictable to think too far ahead. Rather it suggests some possible changes to the way we think about education and training based on taking stock of what is happening right before our eyes. Heutagogy is a stimulus to thinking differently about learning, teaching and education and training and hopefully will assist in generating new thinking about educational practice.

Game changers in education

Taking the role of Nostradamus has always been fraught with danger: even more so given the rapid rate of change that we see in the twenty-first century. However, there are a few reasonably obvious signs of, if not things to come, then trends that should be stimulating the creative juices of those in education and training.

Education systems and institutions are by their very nature conservative. They are slow to change. However, there is a 'game changer' afoot that is hard to ignore and it is the rapid rise of communications technology with instant access to information and the capacity to personally interact with multiple locations almost anywhere on the globe, at any time. No longer does the learner have to be on site in front of teacher. The learner is anywhere on earth, and the class consists of anyone who wishes to join, when they wish to join it: the 'classroom' forms around an issue, a question, an idea and of need. The learner is at the centre of his or her own learning.

The 'now' generation don't want to wait to find things out when they have a need, the motivation to seek. Using their wireless devices they can search the internet, read the latest research, listen to the latest talks on topics via TED or YouTube and follow opinion. If the 'student' needs information to be deciphered or clarified in some way they can search out a facilitator, an expert. Alternatively they can talk to their colleagues or friends, a major source of learning for people, even in traditional education settings.

The twenty-first century is seeing the advent of flexible timeframes that conclude when proof of competence and capability can be demonstrated. The notion that people learn things at the same rate and achieve equivalent levels of ability at the same time is no longer sustainable. The gaining of competence or capability is focused more on need.

As Yrgo Engestrom (2009) posits, the outcome of learning may not be immediately apparent, thus we need to be thinking of learning as emergent rather than predictable or somehow driven. Engestrom also says that the boundaries between disciplines will become even more blurred and need to be managed carefully.

One can only assume that information technology will become ever more effective and more user-friendly. As a friend recently suggested, for the millennium generation, experience does not really exist until it has been communicated through a social media site of some sort. We can be sure that more sophisticated social media experiences will be created and the hardware will be simpler and more accessible. Maybe, to some extent, this is almost a regression to childhood when, prior to school, learning was immediately tied to experience. With the internet there is no formally organized education or curriculum, it is based on what is happening here and now. It is natural, self-determined learning: heutagogy in action.

It seems we are still preoccupied with the national curricula at a time when we need, increasingly, to be thinking about the individual curricula. We are in an age when knowing how to learn and to be a critical thinker are essential to function in modern workplaces, in modern society. Certainly there is a need for essential knowledge and skills but we also need to respond to the way in which people learn, the decreasing boundaries between knowledge areas, the mixed expertise that people often need and motivation to learn. Increasingly people are seeking knowledge but in relation to their specific context.

The rise of neuroscience is likely to transform psychology and, hence, those professions such as education that are dependent on it. New technology has been able to observe in real time what happens in the brain when humans engage in mental activities. This technology is likely to become even more sophisticated and the mysteries of human behaviour will be revealed. We will have a more complete understanding of what actually happens when we learn and, hence, how learning may be enhanced. As a result, very specific methods for learning particular skills and acquiring particular knowledge will be developed, and learning could be accelerated.

These game changers will result in the disappearance of the lecture, the formal discussion group, the lesson plan and the one-day training programme, to be replaced by evidence-based processes that are more learner-centric. Communities of practice or some variation of this concept will be a variation of the classroom mediated perhaps by an expert while knowledge is obtained from the internet and experience.

Changing educational policy and practice

This envisaged future has important implications for the way in which policy-makers and practitioners think about education. In fact, heutagogy challenges some of the old, fixed assumptions about teacher-centric education that have been around since schooling became institutionalized.

We need to be thinking about a more flexible system that takes into account the realities about how people really learn as described in the chapters of this book. Thus, policy-makers should be thinking about what teaching institutions need to look like. They may not consist of walled classrooms around a quadrangle. It is surprising, for example, to still see universities insisting on spending huge amounts of money on infrastructure and cramming more and more students into lecture theatres when this is not where and when people truly learn.

I heard a story recently where a lecturer in a university ordered his students to close their computers and other devices while in his class to that they would listen to him. How different his classroom could have been had he got them to use their devices to explore the concepts his course dealt with rather than put his students into a trance within minutes. He could also have become a co-learner and even enthused himself.

The notion of the individual as the learner as opposed to the teacher-centric national curriculum will be a very controversial issue for many policy-makers and administrators. It is much easier when one has mass education in mind to teach to one syllabus using one method and fixed assessment. There will be even more of an issue when accreditation is involved, as the boundaries between disciplines become blurred when people seek very specific competencies they require. The response to this challenge might be to think in terms of the mastery of competencies and demonstrating capability, rather than on the mastery of content.

The same challenges exist for practitioners of how the 'classroom' or training room might be re-engineered to align with our rapidly changing society. Some innovative approaches to addressing these challenges have been described in this book. Many of these innovations are in the area of online learning, which is not surprising given that it is a new frontier that embraces the very technology that is changing the way many people learn.

The same innovative thinking needs to be applied to face-to-face learning. There is an opportunity to create a hybrid model that uses internet, social communication, lived experience and face-to-face interaction. Some of our contributors have already embarked down this path and are finding the journey very rewarding.

Further exploration and activity

If you would like more ideas about how to use self-determined learning, an internet search will provide you with hundreds of entries. You can also email the authors directly:

stewart.hase@gmail.com and chriskenyon136@gmail.com

You can also visit the Heutagogy Community of Practice website to exchange ideas and experiences, see what's going on with regard to self-determined learning and perhaps post a blog. The address is: http://heutagogycop.wordpress.com.

References

Engestrom, Y. (2009), 'From learning environments and implementation to activity systems and expansive learning', *Actio: An International Journal of Human Activity Theory*, 2, 17–33.

Index